£4·25

D0119578

George Ashby's Poems

EARLY ENGLISH TEXT SOCIETY

Extra Series, No. 76

1899 (reprinted 1965)

PRICE 30s.

George Ashby's Poems

EDITED BY

MARY BATESON

Published for
THE EARLY ENGLISH TEXT SOCIETY
by the
OXFORD UNIVERSITY PRESS
LONDON   NEW YORK   TORONTO

FIRST PUBLISHED 1899
REPRINTED 1965

𝕰xtra 𝕾eries, No. 76

ORIGINALLY PRINTED BY
RICHARD CLAY & SONS LTD., BUNGAY, SUFFOLK
AND NOW REPRINTED LITHOGRAPHICALLY IN GREAT BRITAIN
AT THE UNIVERSITY PRESS, OXFORD
BY VIVIAN RIDLER, PRINTER TO THE UNIVERSITY

INTRODUCTION.

No fresh light is thrown on the history of George Ashby by the publication of these poems, for the few biographical notices they contain have already appeared in print. The first poem was written in the Fleet Prison, 1463, and Ashby describes himself therein as for forty years writer to the Signet. The "Active Policy," written for young Edward, Prince of Wales, "gallant-springing, brave Plantagenet," was penned when Ashby was "right nigh at mony yeres of foure score," and in the preface he describes himself as late Clerk of the Signet[1] to Queen Margaret of Anjou. The facts of Ashby's life, so far as they are known, are recorded in the *Dictionary of National Biography*. A reference, however, may be added to a letter from Margaret of Anjou, 1447—1454, in which she thanks a lady unnamed for her service to "our servant George Ashby, Clerk of our Signet." It is thought that the lady may have been Alice, Duchess of Suffolk, the possible granddaughter of Geoffrey Chaucer,[2] whom Ashby praises in his "Active Policy."

The young Edward, Prince of Wales (1453—1471), must have been a model of virtue if he carried out all Ashby's instructions. These are not dangerously original, but between the lines of Ashby's platitudes we may read something of the peculiar character of the period. Ashby hints at the "great changes of high estates," at much division, due entirely to covetousness. In "Time Present" he

---

[1] Coke, Second Inst., p. 556 [Artic. sup. Cartas, cap. vii.], says, "At the making of this Statute (28 Ed. 1) the king had another seal, and that is called 'Signettum,' his Signet. This seal is ever in the custody of the Principal Secretary ; and there be four Clerks of the Signet, called 'Clerici Signetti,' attending on him. The reason wherefore it is in the Secretaries' custody, is, for that the King's private Letters are signed therewith. Also the duty of the Clerk of the Signet is to write out such Grants or Letters Patent as pass by Bill signed (that is, a Bill superscribed with the Signature or Sign Manual, or Royal hand of the King) to the Privy Seal ; which Bill being transcribed and sealed with the Signet, is a Warrant to the Privy Seal, and the Privy Seal is a Warrant to the Great Seal."

[2] *Letters of Margaret of Anjou*, ed. C. Monro, Camden Society, p. 114.

recommends Edward "all rebellion for to suppress," and, in "Time Future," to put down "false conspirators," and all persons "pretending right to your coronacion"; "grete batellis dispiteous" are named, but it seems scarcely possible that Ashby should write so prosily as he does if another king was in fact reigning in Henry's stead. It is difficult, therefore, to decide at what date this work was written, whether before the Fleet imprisonment, in perhaps 1460-1, or later, perhaps after the reconciliation of Warwick and Margaret, and the temporary Lancastrian successes of 1470.

Ashby appears to have felt a decided respect for history, and constantly recommends Edward to consider what will be said about him in chronicles. Many warnings are given, which may well have arisen from the example of Henry's misfortunes. He presses the claims of old servants (and from his Reflections, he seems to have been one of the neglected); as to money matters, he recommends strict keeping of accounts, and the payment of servants' wages, that they may not resort to extortion; the king must enrich his subjects, but keep himself always the richest;[1] men of high rank should not be treasurers, as the poorer the man the smaller will be his pay. In the choice of ministers Ashby has advice to give; he recommends a councillor, leech, and secretary; in choosing servants, the king should notice with whom they have been brought up; he is to avoid making many lords; he must be careful in granting fees and offices, and he must not withdraw grants after they have been made. Ashby's recommendations on the manner in which petitions should be dealt with indicate some of the abuses which then prevailed. But he was no great reformer, and his motto is not "Trust the people." He bids Edward beware of the commonalty : they must be disarmed, owing to the misuse they make of their arms in private warfare. Maintenance and livery of course are mentioned; compulsory archery is advocated, as also the enforcing of sumptuary laws, and the revival of cloth-making. The king must cherish strangers, pilgrims, and merchants; he is to learn practical economy in buying up goods when they are cheap and in season, and when he can look about him at his leisure. As a Lancastrian he is specially recommended to magnify his ancestry. Ashby approved, we may suppose, of Margaret's peace policy, for he urges great caution in making war. A king ought to study the past history of disturbed

---

[1] Henry's policy was the reverse. Cf. Plummer's *Fortescue*, p. 12.

foreign possessions, so that he may learn what has always been their attitude in the past.

In his diplomatic teaching, Ashby inculcates such a policy as that which Henry VII put into practice. Tale-tellers are not to be too soon credited, but the tale may be borne in mind, and proof amassed to test its trustworthiness. But it must be confessed that Ashby's instructions have, as a rule, no personal interest, and are only of general application.

The "Dicta et opiniones diversorum philosophorum" were evidently drawn from the same original as that used by De Thignon-ville for his French version, which Stephen Scrope and Lord Rivers translated into English. A copy of the Latin version is in MS. ccxli., 127 *b*, Corpus Christi College, Oxford. Stephen Scrope, stepson of Sir John Fastolf, translated the sayings for that knight's contemplation and solace (Harl. MS. 2266), and a copy was corrected after the original (Cambridge Univ. Lib. Gg. i. 34) by William Worcester in 1472. Lord Rivers' translation was printed by Caxton in 1477. There is evidence that these commonplaces had extra-ordinary popularity in the Middle Ages, but the true origin of this collection of proverbs is still to seek.

Since these poems were in type, Prof. Max Förster has edited the Prisoner's Reflections in *Anglia*, 1897, and some interesting notes on scansion enrich his edition. It is hoped that the present edition of the works of Ashby may prove useful to students of fifteenth-century grammar. My best thanks are due to Miss K. Jex-Blake, of Girton College, for her help in the interpretation and emendation of the scribe's Latinity. I am also indebted to Miss J. E. Kennedy for notes and corrections in the English passages, and to Dr. Furnivall for the side-notes to the *Dicta*, and for the List of Words.

Mary Bateson.

CONTENTS.

George Ashby's Poems.

I. A Prisoner's Reflections, A.D. 1463.

MS. R. 3. 19, Trin. Coll. Camb., leaf 41 a.

Prohemium vnius Prisonarii.

(1)

[A]t the ende of Somer, when wynter began   1
  And trees, herbes and flowres dyd fade,
Blosteryng and blowyng the gret wyndes than
  Threw doune the frutes with whyche they were lade,
  Levyng theym sone bare / of that whyche they hade,
    Afore myghelmas, that tyme of seasoñ,
    I was commyttyd, geynst ryght and reasoñ,   7

(2)

In to a pryson, whos name the Flete hight,   8
  By a gret commaundment of a lord,
To whom .I. must obey for hys gret myght,
  Though .I. cannat therto sadly acord,
  Yet .I. must hyt for a lessoñ record,   12
    Ther'yn abydyng without help singler,
    Sauf of god and hys blessyd modyr' ther'.   14

(3)

But oth, or other declaracioñ,   15
  Coude at no seasoñ be herd ne takyñ,
By no prayer ne exhortacioñ.
  But of all pite and grace forsakyñ,
  Myne enemyes on me awakyñ,   19
    Takyng awey hors, money, and goodes,
    Pullyng myne houses downe and gret wordes.[1] 21

        [1] *Sic* in MS.   ? woodes.

ASHBY.   B

(4)

Spoliacio Prisonarii.
His spoliation.

Because of my draught and my bryngyng vp 22
 I haue suffryd thys and other spoylyng,
Nat leuyng me worth a dyssh, neyther cup,
 Of asmoche as myght come to theyr' handlyng,
 Puttyng on me many fals lesyng, 26
  Whyche I must suffyr and bere on my ruge,[1]
  Tyll the trouth discussyd hath god or the iuge. 28

(5)

Nomen Prisonarii.
Name of the prisoner.

George Asshby ys my name, that ys greued 29
 By enprysonment a hoole yere and more,
Knowyng no meane there to be releued,
 Whyche greveth myne hert heuyly and sore,
 Takyng hyt for my chastysement and lore, 33
  Besechyng god I may take my dysease
  In dew pacience, our' lord god to please. 35

(6)

[leaf 41 b.]
Lamentacio prisonarii.
His lamentation on the way he is treated by his friends.

Oon thyng among other greueth me sore 36
 That myne old acqueintaunce disdeyned me
To vysyte, / though I haue doon to theym more
 Kyndnes, / forgetyng me and let me be,
 Ne yeuyng me comfort, ne wold me se, 40
  Ne the werkes of mercy remembryng,
  Ne my kyndnes to theym before shewyng. 42

(7)

He cannot get out of debt.

The grettest peyne that .I. suffyr of all 43
 Is that .I. am put to vnpayable det,
Lykly to be therfore a wrechyd thrall,
 For the enprisonment that .I. am in set,
 Without goddes grace wol hyt souner let. 47
  Wher'opon to god .I. clepe, call and cry
  To help me out of det or .I. dy. 49

(8)

What may I. do ? to whom shall I compleyñ ? 50
 Or shew my trouble, or myne heuynes ?
Beyng in prysoñ, wrongfully certeyñ ;
 But with dylygence and gret besynes,
 I beseche god of hys gret worthynes, 54

      [1] back.

Me to guyde and rewle to hys most plesaunce,
And of my wrong to haue humble suffraunce.   56

(9)

I gan remembre and revolue in mynde   57   *Seruicium*
                                                        Prisonarii.
  My bryngyng vp from chyldhod hedyrto,   His early
                                                        history.
In the hyghest court that I coude fynd,
  With the kyng,[1] quene,[2] and theyr vncle also,
  The duk of Gloucetre, god hem rest do,   61   Kindness of
                                                      Humphrey,
    With whome .I. haue be cherysshyd ryght well,   Duke of
                                                      Gloucester.
  In all that was to me nedefull euery dell.   63

(10)

Wrytyng to theyr' sygnet full fourty yere,   64   Writer to
                                                       the Signet.
  Aswell beyond the see as on thys-syde,
Doyng my seruyce aswell there as here,
  Nat sparyng for to go ne for to ryde,
  Hauyng pen and Inke euyr at my syde,   68
    Redy to acomplysshe theyre commandment,
  As truly as .I. coude to theyr' entent.   70

(11)

And in theyr seruyce I spendyd all my youth,   71   [leaf 42 a.]
  And now in pryson throwen in myn age,
Hauyng of me no pyte ne routh,   Cruel treat-
                                                       ment.
  Reuylyng me with vnfyttyng langage,
  As thaugh I were neyther wytty ne sage,   75
    Whiche greuyd me sore and was gretly sad,
  To be in pouert and of goodes bad,   77

(12)

That before was well in goodes and rest,   78   His former
                                                       good fortune
  And no man was ayenst me dysplesyd,
And all my dayes was among the best.
  And so no creature me dyseasyd,
  But at all tymes with me were pleasyd,   82
    Thaugh fortune lyft make me ryght sory
  Shewyng that thys welth ys transytory.   84

(13)

Gef I had in youth suffred any payne,   85
  By lake of goodes or takyng hardnes,

---

[1] Henry VI.   [2] Margaret of Anjou.

makes his
fall harder to
bear.

I myght the better from tene[1] me refreyne,
And take my fall the better in swetnes.
God for hys hyghe grace and gret worthynes   89
   Counseyll me in my trobyll for the best,
   That I may leue hens in quyet and rest.   91

(14)

Now me-thynketh[2] well, yef I had ben euyr   92
   In prosperyte and in worldly ioy,
And theryn to haue abydyn leuyr
   Then to haue tastyd of thys peynfull noy,[3]
   I cast[4] me nat to be neyther styll ne coy,   96
   But say as me-thynketh, in verray soth.
   To haue chaungyd my lyf I had be loth.   98

(15)

Desires to
lead the best]
life even
though it be
painful.]

And my wrechydnes nat[5] to know euyn,   99
   So well as by goddes grace I shall
And the best lyfe take & the wors leuyn,
   In consyderall that I am mortall,
   And so to obey hym that ys eternall,   103
   And to chaung my lyf to god greable,
   Both in pacyence and in feyth stable.   105

(16)

[leaf 42 b.]

Knowyng in serteyn that my punysshyng   106
   Is other-whyle for my soule profytable,
For a feth in goddes vengeance ceasyng,

The punish-
ments of God
are good.

Vnto goddes plesure ryght acceptable,
   By meke pecyence to vertu able,   110
   Therfore punysshment ys other-whyle good,
   Aswell to low degre as to hygh blode.   112

(17)

I thynke to wryte of trouble rehersall,   113
   How hyt may be takyn in pacyence,
Procedyng theryn for myn acquytall,
   Though I haue no termes of eloquence,
   With that I may conclude perfyte sentence;   117

---

[1] grief. [2] Before thynketh *thyg* struck out.
[3] nay *in MS.*, noye, suffering, annoyance. [4] design.
[5] MS. na.

Wherfore I counseyll attyr wordes thyse,

Eue*r*y man to be lernyd on thys wyse. 119

Writes to counsel patience

*Ad sustinend*um *pacienciam in ad*ue*rsis.*

(18)

O thow creature of nature ryght noght ! 120

Rcmembre thy sylf, thy lyfe, thy demert,

Yef thow to pryson or trouble be broght,

Haply by gret wrong and nat of desert,

Suffryng iniury and ryght peynfull smert, 124

Kepe pacience and wyte[1] hyt thyne offence,

Nat for that sylf thyng but of iust sentence. 126

to those in undeserved trouble,

(19)

Or pe*r*auenture thow mayst ryght-fully 127

Come to trouble or tribulacion.

Yet I counseyll the, suffyr hyt wylfully,

W*ith*out fenyng or simulacion,

Nat the exaltyng by elacion. 131

And thus pacience may the woll p*r*ese*r*ue

From gostly sorow, yef[2] thow thys obse*r*ue. 133

and to those who deserve it.

(20)

And so, by process of suffraunce long, 134

Thow mayst atteyne to ve*r*rey knowlege

Of thy demeryt, and vengeance p*r*olong

By thy lamentyng and prayer mekeleche.[3]

And so at last comfort haue trewleche 138

Aswell here as hense, by godd*es* hyghe grace,

And pe*r*auenture w*ith*-in lytyll space. 140

(21)

And as p*r*ecyous gold ys thorougȟ puryd 141

By foull metall led, and claryfyed,

Ryght so ys the sowle by trowbyll curyd,

And by humble profe, hygh gloryfyęd,

As in the scrypture[4] ys specyfyed. 145

So for soules heltȟ hyt ys a gret grace,

To haue here trouble rather then solace. 147

[leaf 43 a.]

As gold is purified, so is the soul.

---

[1] impute.   [2] MS. yet.   [3] meekly.
[4] Zech. xiii. 9. Jer. vi. 30.

(22)

What ys trouble or trybulacyon,   148
  Vexed wrongfully, or worldly disease,
Lyuyng here without consolacioñ,

    But callyng of god hymself for to please ?
    Wherfore hyt ys best, for thy soules ease.   152
     Rather of trouble be mery and glad,
     Than therof be grogyng,[1] heuy & sad.   154

(23)

Who may haue more heuynes & sorow   155
  Then to be welthy and aftyr nedeful ?
Furst to be ryche, aftyr, redy to borow ?
    Furst prosperous and aftyr carefull ?   158
    Who ys more comfortable and ioyfull ?
     Then take the world iu pacyence and worth,
     Suffryng hit to come and goo playnly forth.   161

(24)

Set the neuyr thy full wyll here   162
  In worldly ioy and in felycyte.
For all dayes thow mayst both see and here,
  In all thy lyfe there ys contraryte ;
    Yef thow be ryche thow hast aduersyte,   166
     Yef thow haue a feyre wyfe and gret plente,
     Moche sorow peraventur' ys sent the.   168

(25)

Yef thow tak a wyfe to thy freelte,   169
    Ryght thoutfull thow art, carfull and pensyf ;
Yef thow lyue aftyr censualyte,
  That ys acursyd and vnthryfty lyf ;
    Yef thow be weddyd, without any stryf,   173
     Thow lakkest chyldren, to be thyne heyres,
     Lesyng[2] thy name in market and feyres.   175

(26)

Yef thow haue chyldreñ ryght plenteuously,   176
  Haply suche may be theyr' gouernaunce
That they woll dysplese ryght greuously ;
  Yef thow be set in holy obseruaunce,

---

[1] grudging.   [2] redeeming.

Perauenture thow hast no temperaunce ;   180   Everything goes by contraries.
   Yef thow be set in temporalyte,
   Thy lust ys in spyrytualyte.   182

(27)

Yef thow be well,[1] haply thow lackest good,   183
   Yef thow haue good, thow suffrest gret sekenes.
Thus welth ebbeth and floweth as the flood,
   Neuer welthy, but som maner dystres,
    Neuyr so mery but som heuynes.   187
     Oone thyng lakkyng aftyr thyne apetyte,
     Nat all thynges beyng in pleasaunt plite.   189

(28)

Yef thow be forth[2] at large out of pryson,   190   There are sorrows outside of prisons.
   Thow mayst haue sorow ynowgh[3] and gret wrong.
Yef thow be ryght welthy for the seson,
   Many pluckers-at thow mayst haue and strong.
   Prosperyte here shall neuer endure long.   194
    So euyr, whyle thow art on erth lyuyng,
    Som maner thyng lakketh to thy plesyng.   196

(29)

Wenest thow to haue here perfeccion   197   No perfection on earth.
   Of worldly ioy, comfort and delyces ?
Nay bettyr ys sharp persecucion
   For thy synnes, offenses and vyces,
    Kepyng pacience without malyces,   201
     Puttyng thy wyll to goddes volunte,
     So thy spyryt may best in quyet be.   203

(30)

Thynke that thy lyfe here ys but pilgremage   204   Life a pilgrimage.
   Towardes the hygh place celestiall.
Wherfore, for any trouble or damage,
   Preve nat thysylf lewde and eke bestiall,
    Seyth[4] thou may be in heuyn menyall   208
     Seruaunt thorough thy tryumphall victory
     By mekenes and werkes merytory.   210

---

[1] MS. *be scke* written as one word.
[2] *be forth* written as one word in MS.
[3] Written as two words in MS.   [4] Sith.

(31)

[leaf 44 a.] Thow canst nat be so pryve ne secret   211
    But god ys there present and knoweth all thyng,
Therfore be euyr wytty and dyscret,
    Nat for to do ne say hym dysplesyng,
But as thow woldest before hym beyng,   215
    So by mekenes take all thyng for the best,
    What that god sendeth, trouble or vnrest.   217

(32)

Thynke that worldes welth and felycyte   218
    Ys nat euermore in oone abydyng,
But transitory ys prosperyte,
Fortune's wheel.   And no certeynte whyle thow art lyuyng.
But euyr as a whele, turnyng and meuyng,   222
    Knowyng for certayñ that thow art mortall,
    And neuer in thys world verray rest haue' shall. 224

(33)

Wytnes of oure lord, allmyghty Ihesu,   225
Sufferings of Christ,   Suffryng Reproves and vexacioñ,
Thowgh he were clennest in lyf and vertu,
    Yet no man suffred suche trybulacioñ.
And all was for our' alther[1] saluacioñ.   229
    Yeuyng vs example for to take trouble
    In worth, syth he hath suffred the double.   231

(34)

of the Virgin, What suffred Mary the quene of heuyñ? 232
    Most pure, most clennyst, without any syñ,
Claryfyed from the synnys seuyñ,
    Ever to plese Ihesu she wold nat blyñ.[2]
How be hyt that feare and tene she was in,   236
    Mornyng, sorowyng, euyr in drede,
    To opteyne the loue of Ihesu and hyr mede.   238

(35)

of St. John the Evangelist, and St. John the Baptist, What sey ye of seynt Iohñ the Euaungelist? 239
    Of many martyrs and eke confessours,
Of holy vyrgyns, and seynt Iohñ Baptist?
    That here in thys lyfe suffred many shours,[3]

[1] Of us all.   See p. 16.   [2] cease.
[3] conflicts.

Nat desyryng therof worldly succours, 243
 Refusyng all worldly ioy and plesaunce,
 And all trowble for god take in sufferaunce. 245

(36)

Of Iob to suffyr take thow example, 246   [leaf 44 *b*.]
 Whyche pacyently suffred hys gret smert,   of Job,
Who had in thys world of losse more ample?
 Yet for god*des* sake he plesyd in hert
 W*ith* hys trowbelous hurt / put out in desert 250
  As fowle, vyle, abhomynable and wreche,
  Takyng hyt in gre[1] and therof nold reche.[2] 252

(37)

And so to procede in the pacience 253
 Of seynt*es*, and make therof rehersall
That suffred trowbyll w*ith* out resystence,
 They be infynyte to be wretyñ all.   of the saints,
 Hyt suffyseth to touche the principall, 257 less.
  To thy lernyng and informacioñ
  To be of pacyent condicioñ. 259

(38)

Rigħt so kyng, Quene, Duke, Prynce and Empe*r*oures,
 Erle, Baroñ, lord, knygħt, and many squyers,
Bysshop, Abbot, Pryo*u*r and conquerours,
 And many gret estates and Rewlours,
 Clerk*es*, marchaunt*es* and eke counseylours 264
  Haue be put in trouble and gret greuaunce
  For theyr' soules helth by humble sufferaunce. 266

(39)

Was there euyr lord so gret and so sure, 267 All classes
 Or any gret Clerk lernyd in the law,   of men have
That may not fall in the snare and in the lure had trouble,
 Of trouble, maugre hys hed and his maw?
 Wherfore hyt may be a lawdabyll saw, 271
  Eue*r*y man worshyp god in hys seasoñ
  Accordyng to hys law / trouth and reasoñ. 273

---

    [1] pleasure.   [2] reck.

(40)

the learned
can teach us
to bear it.

Euery man may take example and hede   274
  By suche men of good disposicioñ,
And by lernyd men that can teche and rede
  To conforme[1] hym to lyk affeccioñ,
  To haue of pacience perfectioñ,   278
    To take trouble in worth and in gre,
    As other men haue do in liberte.   280

(41)

[leaf 45 *a*.]

In conclusioñ of the verrey trouth,   281
  Euery mañ other fauour' and socour',
And of hys trouble haue pyte and routh,
  And the blessyd men helpe and eke honoure,
  Doyng your' dylygence and peynfull laboure,   285
    The virtuous pepyll for to cherysshe,
    Suffryng the wykkyd Rather to perysshe.   287

(42)

That all pacience, Riches and science   288
  Come oonly of god and nooñ other',
Hyt may be prouyd by experience.

Unequal
riches.

  As oone ryche, another pore ; hys brother,
  The ryche, slepeth, the pore laboreth vnder'. 292
    So that Ryches commeth nat by labour
    Oonly / but to hym that god lyst shew fauour. 294

(43)

A prayer.

And syth all thynges come of Ihesu   295
  And nothyng without hym may avayle,
I beseche hym so full of vertu
  To guyde me, Rule me / and counsayle,
  That by pacience .I. may wyn batayle   299
    Of my troubles, and haue the vyctory,
    Thorough my symple werkes merytory.   301

(44)

And with humylyte and soburnes,   302
  With feruent loue and feythfull reuerence,
I beseche the, god, of thy worthynes,
  Yeue me grace, comfort and assistence,
  Good wyll, good werkes, good thought and eloquence,

---

[1] The *m* has an extra stroke.

W*ith* loue, charyte and feyth the to please,
That I may dwell in heuyñ at myñ ease. Amen.

(45) *Lenuoy.*

Goo forth, lytyll boke, mekely, w*ith*out rous,[1]   309
    To folk troubelyd and vexed greuously,
Steryng theym by thy counseil v*er*tuous
    To kepe pacience the*r*eyñ ioyously,
Redyng thys tretyse forth ceryously,   313
    By the whyche they shall fynde grace as .I suppose,
    To comfortable entent and purpose ;   315

(46)

Besechyng all folk, though I am no Clerk,   316   [leaf 45 *b*.]
    For to vndyrstand that I nat p*r*esume   Apology for
To take opon me labo*ur* of thys werk   writing this poem.
    For worldly glory and thank to assume,
    But v*er*tu to encrese and lewdnes consume,   320
        And namely to take trowble in suffraunce
        Paciently to des*er*uyd penaunce.   322

(47)

Also vndyr protestacioñ   323
    That I wyll nat kepe p*r*esumptuosly
Any errou*r*' or feynyd opinioñ,
    But me to theym̄ conforme graciously,
    That of hygh connyng haue plenteuously,   327
        Besechyng theym̄ my defaut to correct,   He is open to
        Yef any be, and nat to me hyt to arect,[2]   329 correction.

(48)

But my dylygence and good wyll to accept   330
    In to theyre fauo*ur*, support and goodnesse,
And in no man*er* me therof except,
    Though .I. haue offendyd in my lewdnesse,[3]
    Vnaduised and nat of wylfulnesse,   334
        Kepyng eu*er*more v*er*tuous entent
        W*ith* discrecioñ that god hath me sent.   336

(49)

Wretyñ in prysoñ, in oure lord*es* date,   337 Written in
    A thowsand foure hundryd syxty and thre,   the Fleet, A.D. 1463.

---

[1] boasting.   [2] impute.   [3] ignorance.

Thus occupying me, thys was my fate,
  Besechyng the, our' lord god in trynyte,
    To take my makyng in plesure and gre,   341
    And therto hau mannys benyuolence,
      To thyne owne preysyng, laude and reuerence.
      Amen.   343

(50)

Explicit.

Remarks
on Prison.

Pryson properly ys a sepulture   344
  Of lyuyng men, with strong lokkes thereoñ,
Fortyfyed without any Rupture,
  Of synners a gret castigacioñ,
  Of feythfull frendes a probacioñ,   348
    Of fre liberte a sharp abstinence,
    Lackyng volunte for theyr' dew penaunce.   350

II. 𝔄𝔠𝔱𝔦𝔟𝔢 𝔓𝔬𝔩𝔦𝔠𝔶 𝔬𝔣 𝔞 𝔓𝔯𝔦𝔫𝔠𝔢.

MS. Mm. IV. 42, leaf 2 *a*, Cambridge University Library.

George
Ashby, late
Clerk of the
Signet to
Queen
Margaret,

[P]resens Libellus compilatus, extractus et anglicatus in Balade per Georgium Asshby, nuper Clericum Signeti Suppreme domine nostre Margarete, dei gratia Regine Anglie, etc. ex bona voluntate, Amore et cordiali affeccione, quos ipse naturali iure gerit, tam erga celsitudinem & regiam maiestatem suam & prepotissimum et

written for
Edward,

excellentissimum dominum suum Edwardum, eadem gratia suppremi domini nostri Regis Henrici et eiusdem

Prince of
Wales.

regine Consortis filium progenitum, principem wallie, ducem Cornubie, et comitem Cestrie, pro cuius amore et complacencia fit ista compilacio . . . . . (*illegible*) suum nobilem Sanguinem, sub quo Ipse a iuuentute sua hucusque & nunquam tota vita sua in alio seruicio

To be divided
into three
parts: Past,

fuit tentus (?) et nutritus. Dividitur in tribus temporibus, videlicet in tempore preterito, presenti & futuro. Tempus preteritum exortatur, sepius meminire de rebus preteritis, ita bene in legendo sacram scripturam et Cronica, sicut alias speculaciones & experiencias . . . .
. . . . . Ipse potest perfecte condere bonorum factorum

bonitatem & opinione*m* libror*um*. Et miserimam ruinam
malefactor*um* & misero*rum*, . . . nde se sapienter &
felicit*er* gub*er*nare. Tempus p*re*sens facit quomo*do*   Present,
se gerriet (*sic*) i*n* sapiencia & pollecia deo placenti-
b*us* & p*o*p*u*lis suis & pro suimet ipsius securitate.
Tempus futurum p*ro*uidet discrete & prudenter p*ro*   and Future.
reb*us* futuris . . . . diendo se in honor*e* beata fama et
bona gubernitate et euitando dampna vituperia et in-
conueniencia . . . . etiam fore activu*m* in pollecia et sapiencia . . . . subditor*um* securitate & bona custodia sub
debita et fideli obediencia per aduisamenta edicta &   Opinions of Philosophers.
opiniones diu*er*soru*m* Philosophor*um*, quor*um* nomina
. . . in tractatu breuiter subscribuntur. (*Much defaced.*)

Hic Incipit Prologus.

(1)

Maisters Gower, Chauucer & Lydgate,   1   [leaf 2 b.]
Compliment-
ary notice
to Gower,
Chaucer, and
Lydgate.
   Primier poetes of this nacion,
Embelysshing oure englissĥe tendure algate,
   Firste finders to oure consolacioñ
Off fressĥe, douce englissĥe and formacioñ   5   Their use of
English and
new ballad
forms.
      Of newe balades, not vsed before,
      By whome we all may haue lernyng and lore.   7

(2)

Alas ! saufe godd*es* wille, & his plesaunce,   8   Lament over
their death.
   That euer ye shulde dye & chaunge this lyffe,
Vntyl tyme / that by youre wise pourueunce (*sic*)
   Ye had lafte to vs / sum remembratife
      Of a personne, lerned & Inuentif,   12
         Disposed aftur youre condicioñ,
         Of fressĥe makyng to oure Instruccioñ.   14

(3)

But sithe we all be dedly and mortal,   15
   And no man may eschewe this egressioñ,
I beseche almygĥty god eternal   Prayer for
their souls.
   To pardoñ you all / youre transgressioñ,
      That ye may dwelle in heuenly mansioñ,   19
         In recompense of many a scripture
         That ye haue englisshede without lesure.   21

(4)

So I, George Assħby, not comparisoñ 22
Making to youre excellent enditing,
Witħ rigħt humble prayer & orisoñ,
Pray god that by you I may haue lernyng,
And, as a blynde man in the wey blondryng, 26
As I can, I shall now lerne and practise
Not as a master but as a p[r]entise ; 28

(5)

Besechyng almyghti god of support, 29
That thorougħ his gracious instructioñ
I may confourme me aftur the report
Of vertuous / and sad construccioñ,
Without minisshyng or addicioñ, 33
Principally in thentent and substance
Of my matere, with all the obseruance. 35

(6)

And thaugħ all thynges be nat made perfyte 36
Nor swetely englisshed to youre plesance,
I byseche you hertely / to excuse it,
So that I kepe intential substance,
While I haue of makynge none assurance, 40

Nor of balades haue experience,
Acceptyng my goode wille & diligence. 42

(7)

Some personnes peraventure woll thenke 43
That it mygħt be saide better thus or thus.

For I cannat swym / I stand on the brynk,
Wadyng no forther / but as crist Iesus
Sendith me konnyng, showing vnto vs 47
That a litle childe may natt so well bere
A grete burthen / as a man, withoute dere.[1] 49

(8)

Rigħt so thougħ I haue not seien scripture 50

Of many bookes rigħt sentenciall,
In especial of the gloses sure,
I woll therfor kepe true menyng formal,
Nor rigħt meche delatyng[2] the rehersall, 54

[1] injury.   [2] spinning out, dilating.

Thaugh I do nat so wele / as thei before,
Ostendyng my beneuolence & lore, 56

(9)

By protestacioñ that my menyng 57
Shall not be wilfully for to displease
Any creatures to my konnyng,
Principally suche as I aught to please,
Ner their estat in no wyse to displease, 61
But to my pore power / it to magnifie,
And in al my seruice / it to multiplie. 63

He hopes his poem will vex no one.

(10)

Thaugh I be fallen / in decrepit age 64
Right nygh at mony yeres / of foure score
I pray god that in my wytt / I ne rage
But that I may wryte aftur goddes lore,
Encrecyng vertuous liffe more & more, 68
As myne entente is / and also shalbe,
To goddes plesance / & to my dutie. 70

He is nearly eighty,

(11)

Under a support / and beneuolence, 71
With a fauorable direction;
I woll put to[1] / my peine & diligence,
After the simplesse of mine opinion,
To my cunnyng and erudicioñ ; 75
This matier is finisshe to the pleasance,
Of almyghty Iesu & his suffrance. 77

but will do his best.

(12)

In the name of almyghty Lorde Iesu, 78
To whom heuen erth and helle —yne,[2]
Whiche is the grete name / higheste in vertue,
And in all gracious goodenes dothe shyne,
Whom I biseche me for to Illumyne, 82
That in my mater I may so procede
Without offense / & therin not texcede. 84

[leaf 4 a.]

De actiua pollecia principis.

(13)

[R]ight [high] & myghty prince and my right goode Lorde,
Linially comyn of blode royal,

---

[1] *Put to* written in one word.   [2] Illegible.   ? inclyne.

Bothe of Faders & moders of recorde,
  Occupying by grace celestial
  Thaier Roiaulmes, w*ith* grace especial (?)   89
    To whom be al honnour and reuerence,
    Dewe to youre high estate / and excellence,   91

(14)

Dedication to Prince Edward.
I mene, to youre highnesse Edwarde by name,   92
  Trewe sone & heire to the high maiestie (?)
Of oure liege lorde / Kynge Henry & *dame* (?)

Character of his parents.
  Margarete, the Quene / bothe in Charitee
  Euer though grete was their maiestie (?)   96
    Yit they eschewed / vengeance and Rigoure,
    Shewynge their beneuolence and Favour.[1]   98

(15)

[leaf 4 *b*.]
Blessings on them.
God, verrey Recompenser of goodenesse,   99
  Rewarde at large their blessidnesse therfore,
And so I dar say / he wil of his Rightwisnesse ;
  Enlarge theim daily / his grace more & more,
  Blissed be tyme in whiche thei were bore,   103
    Namly for youre birthe of theim discended,
    In whome al vices ben vilipended.[2]   105

(16)

My goode Lorde, trewe hertly affection   106
  Compellithe me somewhat to entremete,[3]
In fyndyng sum goode exhortacion
  That myght be to you / gracious & mete,
  Ensuryng youre estate in quiete sete,   110
    Whiche may neuer endure but by vertue,
    According to the pleasance of Iesu.   112

(17)

Prince Edward's good bringing up.
And so youre bringyng vp hath be right sad,   113
  In all vertuous disposicion,
And to the honnour of god / euer ladde,
  Whome I biseche be youre proteccion,
  That ye may abide in suche affeccion,   117
    Not oonly to youre profite & honnour,
    But als to oure althre[4] wele & socour.   119

---

[1] This verse is damaged.   [2] thought ill of.   [3] intermeddle.
[4] See above, p. 8.

(18)

Besides whiche thre thing*es* I wolde meve   120   Do not forget Time.
  Your high estate to haue in Remembrance,
Kepying (*sic*) theim in youre breste and neuer leue,
  For any busynesse or attendance,
    Puttyng youre high estate in assurance,   124
      That is tyme Passed pr*e*sent and future,
      Kepynge thees three tymes with due mesure.   126
        In tempore preterito.

(19)

[O]f tyme passed I wolde ye sholde take hede,   127   Importance of reading the Bible.
  Redyng the bible & holy scripture,
And there ye may see to what ende dothe lede
  Vertuos dedys & condutes seure,
    Principally suche as haue noble cure,   131
      For certeyne a blissed entencioñ
      Must determine wele withoute questioñ.   133

(20)

And other men, in the contrary wise,   134
  That be indisposed to rightwisnesse[1]
Must nedis fal, and al folk theim dispise,
  Sith their werkes bene without aduisinesse,
    Hauing no regarde to goode stedfastnesse,   138
      And so who so eu*ere* wol preve the sothe,
      He endithe not wele that wykkidly dothe.   140

(21)

Seintes of youre noble blode ye may knowe,   141   Saints his ancestors,
  Diuers many that lyued blessedly,
Bothe of this England and of Fraunce ynowe,   French and English.
  That yave theire her*tes* to god Inwardly,
    Abydy in godd*es* feith stedfastly,   145
      Whos pathes ye may beholde & eke see,
      And theim folowe in theire benignitee.   147

(22)

Beholde eke youre noble progenitours,   148
  Howe victorious thei were in corage,
How Iuste, how sad & eke wise at al houres,
  Holdyng theire enemyes in seruage,

[1] Two words in MS.

ASHBY.   D

So that thei durst nat so hardy outrage,   152
   Whos werkes be cronicled to their fame.
Be suche as thei were, & no man wol you blame.

(23)

Ye may rede in cronicles the ruine   155
   Of high estates and translacioñ,[1]
That to vices and outrage dud incline,
   For the whiche thei suffred mutacion,
Wherof ye haue daili probacion.   159
     For certeine no persoune may longe indure,
     But he attende wele to his charge & cure.   161

(24)

Ther was neuer yet fal / of high estate,   162
   But it was for vices / or negligence,
Were he neuer so high / or eleuate,
   Withoute he wolde attende wele by prudence
To his charge, avoidyng from his presence,   166
     Men vicious, and namely couetous ;
     Where thei abide thei distroy euery hous.   168

(25)

Ther hath be in late daies right grete change   169
   Of high estates and grete diuision,
Right meruelous, wonderful & eke strange
   To myche folk unportable punicion,
Sorouful, peineful, and tribulacion,   173
     Whiche might [haue be] eschewed in this wise,[2]
     To haue had counseil without couetise.   175

(26)

Ther was goode ynough if ther had be hert   176
   To haue departed therwith in all haste,
And saued many a man that toke smert,
   But rather thei wolde take the deth is taste
   Than thei wolde for theimselfe theyr goode oute cast,
     And so loste there maister,[3] theimselfe & goode,
     Oonly couetise shedynge their blode.   182

---

[1] Perhaps the meaning is "and of their transference."
[2] Line much defaced.
[3] Perhaps he alludes to the death of Richard, Duke of York, 1460.

(27)

Howe may any estate be in seurtee 183
  Of his welthe, prosperite & honno*ur*,
Or in any wise be in sikertee,
  If couetous folke be in his favour?
    Whiche people wol do / their peine & labo*ur* 187
      Euer for their owne singularitee,
      Charging no p*er*sonne [h]is aduersitee. 189

Dangers of
covetousness.

(28)

The high estate of oure king god p*r*eserue, 190
  And if deuoided had folke couetous
From his p*er*soune, his people had not sterue
  With suche grete batellis dispiteous,
  Whiche to here & telle is ful piteous. 194
    For to late the couetous folk toke hede
    To haue holpen theim selfe whan it was nede. 196

The late
grievous
battles show
they might
have been
avoided.

(29)

Ful openly shewithe experiens 197
  To what effect couetise drawith to.
It is apte to vntrouthe and negligence,
  To falsenesse and subtel treson also,
  Euer for lucre, go where he go, 201
    Hauyng no regarde to trouthe ne worship,
    So he may come to goode and Lordeship. 203

Sins of the
covetous.

(30)

Who that herith many Cronicles olde, 204
  And redithe other blessid Scripture,
Shall excede al other bi manyfolde
  Resons, and his discrecions ful sure,
  Circumspect in his actes, wytt pure, 208
    And so to guyde hym in siche cases lyke
    As other men dudde that were polletike. 210

History
teaches cir-
cumspection.

(31)

Tempus preterit kepe in youre Remembrance, 211
  And reuolue in youre cogitacion,
How mysruled haue fallen in comberance,
  And wele ruled in exultacion.
  Chese the best for youre consolacioñ, 215

Euer gracious & blissed entent,
Maketh to fynisshe wele youre tyme present. 217

Iam de tempore presenti.

(32)

Tthe (*sic*) god / of his omnipotencie   218
  Hath brought you now forth to *our* grete comfort,
So Iesu encrece you, to Iustifie
  And rule this present tyme for owre support,
    That al people may haue cause to report   222
      The blessednesse of youre estate Roial,
      Pleasyng god and to the wele of vs al.   224

(33)

Edward's opportunity. And also al wronges for to redresse,   225
  With lauful and dewe moderacion,
And all rebellion for to suppresse,
  Aftur Iust & dewe informacion,
    All thing doon with consideracion,   229
      As the case requireth, in his due wise,
      For to youre highnesse is this entreprise.   231

(34)

Suche as ye be, so shall ye be taken,   232
Your works will go down to posterity in history. Youre dedys & werk*es* shal prove al thing,
Wele or evyl thei shalbe awaken,
  In cronicles youre Rule rehersyng,
    Either in preisyng either in blamyng.   236
      Nowe here ye may chese wherto ye wol drawe,
      Best is to confourme you / to goddys lawe. 238

(35)

Goddys lawe is man to knowe his estate,   239
  And goddis wille haue in dewe obseruance,
And his owne Cure if he be fortunate,
  And thise three euer haue in assurance,
    And so shall he his high estate enhaunce, 243
      And his goode dedys be magnified,
      Bothe here and in heuyn glorifieed.   245

(36)

Of magnificence. To entremete / of youre magnificence,   246
  I woll make therof but litil wrytyng,

Aduertising youre estate & excellence
  Not to be to hasty in youre wyrkyng,
  Ne to slowe, ne to feint, for no temptyng,   250
    Ne to riall, ne in to grete simplesse,
    Ne to liberal for no frendlynesse.   252

Duty of moderation.

(37)

Ne ouer streit for noo necessite,   253
  But in a meane bi moderacioñ,
And so youre estate shall encrece & thee,[1]
  And yet thaugh bi consideracioñ,
    Of youre honnour and nominacioñ,   257
    At a point al other ye do excelle,
    Another[2] tyme ye may it .Repelle.   259

(38)

And euer drawe to youre noble seruice   260
  The mooste vertuos folkes and cunnyng,
That may youre entencion accomplice,
  Youre high estate and grete honnour sauyng
  And suche ye may haue that cause no blamyng, 264
    Suche as a man is / suche drawithe hym to,
    Either vertuous folk or therto fo.   266

Choose your servants well.

(39)

And also beware of the couetous,   267
  He is nat for youre profett and honnour,
He shall appere false and sedicious,
  Be al quaint socibbilitees and labour,
    Corruptyng his fellawship bi errour,   271
    Of his false couetous opynion,
    This is verrey soothe withoute questioñ.   273

(40)

Take you to liue of youre own properte   274
  Of youre Revenues, lyuelode & Rent,
Propornouning after the quantite
  Youre expenses by youre oune Iugement,
  Paying all that is to youre estate lent.   278
    Thus ye shall oure lorde god & the world please,
    And all men fayne to leue you at youre ease. 280

Keep within your income

---

[1] thrive.   [2] A nother in MS.

(41)

The wiseman saithe do all thinge with counseil,   281
 Not biddynge youre counsail do al thing,
Right so if ye go youre selfe to batail,
 All folk woll folowe you in youre helpyng.

  Do youre selfe and all shall be obeying,   285
   Truste to no man is execucion,
   So wele as to youre oune inspeccioñ.   287

(42)

Principally I wolde you aduertise,   288
 The thynges to kepe in youre remembrance.
Oon is the vertuous folk to cherisshe
 And þe vicious to put in grevance,
  Disseuering theim bi youre ordynaunce,   292
  Yevyng hym rewarde & other expence,
   According to his merites and desert,
   And thus ye shall avoide euery smert.   295

Docet[1] Regem satisfacere / de stipendiis stipendiariis suis
Alioquin societas despiciet eum & dominium suum ; hec
  Plato.
    (43)

And paie youre men theire wages & dutee,   296
 That thei may lyue withoute extorcion,
And so wol god trouthe & equitee,
 And therfore take hertili this mocion,
  And in their nedys be their proteccion.   300
  And so shal youre fame encrece & rise,
   And euery man youre pleasire accomplise.   302

(44)

Be ye rather clept an executer   303
 Of wisdam, in his deue & formal wise,
Than to be proclamed a wise speker,
 And nought folowethe aftur that guyse,
  Of bothe, weldisposed, fame shal arise,   307
  So youre estate to wisdam do Incline,
   Wherbi al myshappe fallith to Ruine.   309

(45)

All thynges aftur wisedam to gouerne   310
 Is verrey suretee and trusty assurance,

    [1] Perhaps for decet.

And pleasith almyghti Jhesu eterne,
  If ther be put in hym trewe affyance,
  Whiche ye may obserue in youre Remembrance, 314
    That noght eschape in dissolucion,
    Ne wested by delapidacion. 316

(46)

And in al thynges kepe order deuly. 317   Keep order
  What is curtesye, trouthe, Reason, pite
Or Iustice but a true ordre truly?
  All thes vertues returned may be
  To vices, withoute ordre in his degree. 321
    Therfore ordre other' while wol nat speke,
    But in couenable tyme he wol owte breke. 323

(47)

That ye must nedis doo bi rightwisenesse,[1] 324
  Bi trouthe, goode conscience or Iuggement,
Do it with pite & pacientnesse,
  With no vengeance in youre commandement,
  For that longithe to god omnipotent, 328
    And who that is withoute grace and pite,
    At last bi reason he shall vnthe.[2] 330

Fundamentum timoris dei est pietas / hec Pitogoras.

(48)

Pite withoute rightwysnesse is folye, 331   One virtue needs another.
  Rightwisnesse withoute pite tiranshi͞p,
The toon withowte the tother withoute any lye
  May not contynue in myght of Lordeshi͞p,
  But at last it woll come to shenshi͞pp,[3] 335
    Therfore haue herto a goodely respect,
    That ye be not herein founden suspecte. 337

(49)

Yeuethe no light credence to euery tale, 338   Sound advice.
  Ner beleue not euery suggestion,
Nor by not euery thynge that is to sale,
  Ner graunte ye not euery peticion,
  But hauethe ye consideracion 342
    To euery thing, as the cause requirethe,
    Just, trewe, necessarye, as it semythe. 344

---

[1] Two words in MS.   [2] Not thrive.   [3] Ruin.

(50)

Do not pro-
crastinate.

Delay no thyng to be doon bi reason,   345
  Ne deferre it *with*oute cause resonable,
For thing done quykly in his season,
  Is right worthi to be commendable,
  And to al creatours laudable.   349
    Bothe profit and worship shal herby sewe
    To theym p*er*fourmyg (*sic*) it and never rewe. 351

Sitis intra et extra idem ab hiis que loquimini; [1]
ad inuicem ne sit quod linguis exprimitis diversum
ab eo quod reconditis in corde; hec Hermes.

(51)

Say nat oon thyng and do the contrarie,   352
  Lete youre worde & dede be in accordance,

Be secret as
a secretary.

Kepe secretnesse as a secretarye,
  For youre worshippe, proffite and assurance,
  Withoute langage, speche or vtterance,   356
    But vnto suche p*er*sonnes oportune
    As may be furthering to youre fortune.   358

(52)

Hear counsel
patiently.

Heere euery man is counseil & aduise   359
  Paciently & chese therof the best,
And than I wold youre highnesse aduertise
  That ye sholde kepe youre entent in y*our* brest,
  As ye wolde y*our* owne tresoure in youre chest. 363
    And so shall ye youre estate magnifie,
    And youre grete wisdam daily multiplie.   365

(53)

And kepe no selfe-willed oppunion,   366
  But to all reason bethe appliable,
And allowe als *with*oute obliuion,
  Euery man is goode wille / resonable,
  Thaugh y*our* wytt excelle & be more hable   370
    To discerne the vtterest Iugement
    In any case to you app*ur*tenent.   372

[1] The English version runs, "Be all one within and without
in that ye shall speak."

Iam de tempore Futuro.

(54)

[N]ow of two tymes I wol speke no more,   373   The Future.
  It suffiseth, to youre discrecion.
But of futur' temps I wol meve therfore,
  Biseching you / vnder youre proteccion,
    That ye wol take herin Inspeccion.   377
      And kepe it in youre noble remembrance,
      For the web of youre estate and surance.   379

(55)

Be wele ware by discrete prouision   380
  For to suppresse youre false conspiratours,   Conspiracy.
Aftur the lawe & constitucion,
  Established ayenst[1] opyn traiterous,
    Being circumspect as youre progenitours,   384
      In suche caas (*sic*) haue bene to the preseruing,
      Of their Royal estate and preseruyng (*sic*).   386

(56)

Wolde to god that ye wolde prouide sadly   387
  To subdewe al maner rebellyon,   Rebellion,
Namely of suche countreies that gladly
  Be disposed to insurreccion,
    Wherof ye may haue intelleccion   391
      Redyng Cronicles, and then ye may fynde
      Whiche places bene to thair deue kyng vnkynde.

(57)

In euery thyng haueth a prouidence   394
  That no hurt fal to youre noble highnesse,
Not bi conspiryng ner bi necligence,
  Exilyng from you slough & simplenesse,
    In suche thing as sholde sowne[2] to youre distresse,
      Hauyng al waies a tendre regarde,
      to youre seuretee sparing for no Reward.   400

(58)

Almyghty Jhesu was disobeied,   401   Traitors to
  First by Adam and Eve in paradise,   Christ.
Thurgh the fals deuel to theim conueiede,
  And in heuyn by lucifer vnwise,

---
[1] Two words in MS.   [2] tend.

And in erthe bi Iudas in his false guyse.   405
Haue not ye now nede aboute[1] you to loke?
Sith god was deceyvede hy wiles croke.   407

(59)

Be wele ware of falsehode in felawshīp,   408
    And namly of corrupte bloode and suspecte,
Abidyng in power, myght & lordeshīp,
    And be towardes thair rule circumspecte,
    And to thaire werkes haueth respecte,   412
      And if thei trespace Lete not theim eschape,
      Iustly punysshyng then & not with Iape.   414

(60)

Pretenders. Oon thyng I warne you, if ye wol be Kyng,   415
    Thurgh goddes grace, of any Region
Ye must subdewe with al suppressyng
    Euery persoune withoute submission
Pretendyng right to your coronacioñ.   419
      Or ellis ye may not regne in seurte,
      Nor set youre subiettes in quiete.   421

(61)

Old servants. And euer remembre olde Sarueyeres,   422
    Hauyng suche persounes in tendernesse
That hathe be feithfull & trewe welewyllers
    To thair ligeance withoute feintnesse,
Suffryng therfore / grete peine & butternesse (*sic*)
Beware of   And be ye ware of the Reconsiled
reconciled
enemies.   That hathe deserued to be reuiled.   428

(62)

Recent ex- May nat ye see late the experience   429
perience.   Howe falshede, mysreule & extorcion
Mysguidyng, Robbery & necligence,
    Withe all ther wiles haue conclusion
Of destruction and confusion,   433
      Wherto shal we expresse thair proper name,
      That so haue perisshed to thair grete blame?   435

(63)

The trouthe is not hid, ne neuer shalbe,   436
Chronicles   Cronicles faueurithe no man of Reason.

           [1] Two words in MS.

Their disclaundre shal neuer die of equite

do not favour traitors.

    That falsly haue conspired bi treson,

        Or lyued vngodly in iche seasoñ.   440

          Do youre parte as longithe to your highnesse,

          To avoide prudently suche heuynesse.   442

(64)

For truste me, verreyly god wol be knoweñ,   413

    He rewardythe euery benefet,

And punyssheth bothe high & eke the lowe,

    Be he neuer so queinte or countrefet,

        His rightwise Iuggement he neuer let,   447

          Thawe he delay it of his diuine grace,

          For a tyme of better leiser and space.   449

(65)

Muche folke wissheñ hertely to be alorde (*sic*)   450

    For grete plente, worshiƥ & reuerence

Duties of lordship.

Takyng no hede what sholde therto accorde,

    So thai haue thair pleasir and complacens.

        To whiche entent god neuer yaue suche sentence,

          But that thei sholde be in chageabe (*sic*) cure,

          To directe other vndur dewe Mesure.   456

(66)

Also take this for a note and Lesson,   457

    Yf ye be put in high estate & cure,

But ye reule deuly at tyme & seasoñ,

    Accordyng to right, as seithe Scripture,

        A wreche shall reule theim withoute mesure,   461

          To a grete punisshyñg and chastement

          To be at a wreche is commaundent.   463

(67)

Prouide you sadly for youre sowles is helthe   464

Have a Confessor,

    Of a Confessour in discrecioñ,

Of a goode leche for youre body is welthe,

Doctor,

    Of a Secretarie withe Inspectioñ,

Secretary.

        Secrete, sad, and of goode Intencion,   468

          That can accomplisshe your commaundement.

          To thonnour and profit of youre entente.   470

(68)

Also chese y*our* servant*es* of goode draugĥt,   471
    That wol attente and be seruiable,
Remembryng with whom thei haue be vpbraugĥt,
    For to suohe thei shalbe appliable.
        Whether thei be good or nat vailable,   475
            So take herin a goode direccioñ,
            To haue seruice wi*th*oute suspecion.   477

(69)

Looke that youre serv*a*unt*es* be of the best,   478
Bothe Knygĥtes, Squiers, Clercs & yomen,
And eueriche in his degre vertuest
        Whiche shalbe to y*our* glorious fame then,
        In all countrees that men may you ken,   482
            As well in grete strenght, profit & honno*ur*
            As to al youre trewe Soubgett*es* soco*ur*.   484

(70)

Prouide bifore for al thing in seasoñ   485
    In youre estate, householde & other thing,
And ye shall haue better chepe bi reason
        Of youre prouision in the bying,
        Than whan ye may make therof no tarying,   489
            For whan a thing must right nedys be had,
            It must be receiued, goode, chepe or bad.   491

(71)

A peny spent bi wise prouisioñ   492
    Auailith two in time seasonable,
And in lyke wise the execucion
        Of dedys by tyme is right profitable,
Where in taryeng it is mutable,   496
            Therfore some thing*es* oóns by tyme doon
            Ben worthe twyes / other thing ouergoon.   498

(72)

Prouide that y*our* Commun*es* may be welthy,   499
    In richesse, goodes and prosperite,
And to occupacion theim applye,
        Vndur drede of the lawe is Rigourstee.
        For of what condicion that he be,   503

And he be of goodes right plentuous,
He dar not be to lawe contrarious.   505 The comfortable are the most law-abiding.

(73)

For he that nought hathe is nat vnder drede,   506
  Neither of lawe, ne of punicion,
For in other place / he may his nede spede,
  No thing rechyng of transgression,
  Ne willyng to come / to submission.   510
    For he that hathe of goodes no substance,
    He may the soner make than auoydance.   512

(74)

It hathe be, and yet is a comyn sawe,   513 *A proverb.*
  That Poverte departithe felaship.
Therfor vnder rule & drede of the lawe,
  Kepe youre Comyns bi helpe of your lordeship,   *Keep your commons,*
  That they may growe to richesse & worship,   517
    And than at tyme of nede thei may you aide,
    As often sithes as they shalbe praied.   519

(75)

Prouide that lawe may be excercised,   520 *and provide laws*
  And executed in his formal cours,
Aftur the statutes autorised
  By noble Kynges youre progenitours,
  Yeving therto youre aide helpe & socour.   524
    So shall ye kepe folk in subieccion
    Of the lawe and trewe dispocision.   526

(76)

Yif ye wol bryng vp ayen[1] clothe makyng,   527 *to revive cloth making;*
  And kepe youre Comyns oute of ydelnesse,
Ye shull therfore haue many a blessyng,
  And put the pore people in busynesse,
  Bi the whiche thei shal come to grete swetnesse,
    And robbery lafte by that excercise,
    And strumpery als by this entreprise.   533

(77)

Lete nat the pouer Comyns be dysguised   534 *pass sumptuary laws.*
  Nee haue precious clothe in theire Vesture,

---

[1] Two words in MS.

But in thair excesse be ther supprised
　And obserue a resonable mesure
　　In their arraye, w*ith* oute chaunge but tendure,　538
　　　Accordyng to degree of Laborours,
　　　Aftur statute of youre / progenitours.[1]　　540

(78)

Youre Comyns shude nat bere dagger, ne Lance,　541
　Ne noon other wepins defensife,
　　Leste therby thei cause debate & distance,
　　　Yeuynge other occasions / of Striff,
　　　Swhiche wepyns haue made folk to lese their liff.
　　　　And if this statute[2] were executed
　　　　Meche folk sholde be Laufully rebuked.　　547

(79)

Also gentilmen shuld nat yeve clothyng　　548
　But to their howshold meyne, for surance
　　That no man be their power excedyng,
　　　Ne maynteine no people, by youre puissance,
Ner false quarels take thorough maintenance,　552
　　　　But euerry man lyve of his owne in rest,
　　　　And that pleasithe god and man most best.　554

(80)

Euery man ought to lyve vnder a lawe,　　555
　And namly cristenmen that wold god please,
　And for drede therof to lyve under awe.
　　For miscreant*es*, for drede of disease,
　　Bene obedient to their lawe doutelesse,　　559
　　　And muche more rather to be obseruante[3]
　　　Of cristen lawe we shulde yeve attendance.　561

(81)

What region may Lyve w*ith*oute a reule?　562
　Or abide quietly In assurance,
　Thaugh he were an asse hede or a dulle mule,
　　He myght not lyve wildly at his pleasance.
　　But at last ye shall falle in grevance,　　566
　　　As ye may bi experience it se,
　　　Mysruled folk evyll doon thrive or thee.[4]　568

---

[1] 37 Ed. III. c. 8-14.　　　[2] 2 Ed. III. c. 3.
　[3] MS. obseruance.　　　[4] flourish.

(82)

By lawe euery man shold be compellede   569   Compulsory
    To vse the bowe and shetyng for disport,   archery.
And al insolent pleies Repellede,
    And iche towne to haue Buttes for resort   Butts.
    Of euery creature for their comfort,   573
        Especially for al oure defence
        Establisshed before of grete prudence.   575

(83)

Iff any people put to youre highnesse   576   Treatment
    Billes of compleint or peticion   of subjects'
Onswere theim in haste *with* aduisinesse,   petitions.
    Werto they shal trust *with*oute decepcion,
    Aftur the trouthe & Iuste pe*r*feccion   580
        That folke be nat delaied friuolly,
        Otherwyse then the case askith iustly.   582

(84)

My lorde al men shuld be vnder' y*our* drede,   583
    That bene vnder y*our* reule & obeisance.
So must ye vnder god in worde & dede,
    In eschewing his wrathe & displeasance.
    He wol be deled *with* in sad constance,   587
        Neither *with* Iapes, mokke ne scornyng,
        But Iustly, truly, even & mornyng.   589

(85)

No man reuleth god, be (*sic*) he reulith al,   590   The ruling
    Bothe heuen, erthe, and also helle.   of God.
What man is he that is terrestial
    But of hym thus sadly wol speke & telle?
    Al kyng*es* & princes he dothe excelle.   594
        Suche a maister that is worthi & best
        Is surest to serue and at longe moost rest.   596

(86)

And for most espe*c*ial Remembrance   597   You are His
    Thinketh that men be erthly & mortal,   subject.
Ner there is worldly Ioy ne assurance
    But in almyghti Ihe*s*u eternal,
    Bi whos myght & power espe*c*ial,   601
        Reignen kyng*es*, and be to hym soubget,
        And hym to obey is thaire deutee & dette.   603

(87)

Oon thing kepe rigĥt stedfastly in your mynde,   604
    If any man do thinge for youre plasance,
Acquite you ayein[1] of natural kynde,
    Though ye wil nat hym therfore auance,
      Yit lete hym wyt that ye haue therof rememberance,
        Whiche is to hym a sufficiant Reward,
        And ever to please you wol haue regarde.   610

(88)

And als euer amonge cherisshe straungers,[2]   611
    Marchandes, pilgrymes & great Clerkes,
In especial suche as be makers.
    Thise may exaltat youre name & werkes,

    Aftur the oolde dogge the yonge whelpe barkes ; 615
      Study euer to haue men is fauour
      By vertue, or elles lost is youre labour.   617

(89)

Whan any man tellethe you any tale,   618
    Serche it priuely to haue trewe knowlege
Whether it be soothe, and to you no bale,
    And than kepe it in secretnesse treuleche,
      Til ye haue youre ful entente feithfullyche,   622
        And so ye may ful many thynges knowe,
        Where bi blabbynge thei may be overthrowe. 624

(90)

Oon thing kepe in youre noble memorie,   625
    Do magnifie & enriche youre dscent (*sic*),
And thaugh al other ye do modifie,
    I holde it a prouision prudent,
    Lete not theime be to you equiuolent,   629
      Neither in myghti pouer ne Richesse,
      In eschewyng hapley youre oune distresse.   631

(91)

To make many lordys bethe aduised,   632
    But thei be of youre lyue or cause vrgent,
Leest the Realme be charged & supprised,
    And therbi the folke haue cause to repent.
    God hathe you grace and plentuous wit sent,   636

---

[1] Two words in MS.   [2] *Sic* in MS.

Take this lesson to noon obliuion,
For many folke holde this opinion. 638

(92)

Make knyght*es*, squiers & gentilmen riche, 639
And the pore Comyns also welthy,
But to youre richesse make neuer man liche,
If ye wol stande in peas and be set by.
So wol god and polleci sykerly, 643
Lyke as ye in estate other excelle,
In p*ro*pre richesse ye sholde bere the belle. 645

Lessons learnt from Henry VI.

(93)

Yf god sende you children plentuously, 646
As I truste to god he wole right wele,
Do theim to be lettred right famously
Wherby thei shall reule bi Reason and skele,
For leud*e* men litle discrecion fele. 650
Who that is lettred suffician[t]ly,
Rulethe meche *with*oute swerde obeiceantly. 652

Teach your children.

(94)

Satis cito sit quidquid bene[1] *sit.*

Euery day be ware of that extremite 653
Not to be to hasty in mandement,
But medle th[e]rwith youre benignite,
Being to high and lowe Indifferent.
For youre Lawe is to bothe equiuolent, 657
Lyke as al other ye do Rectifie,
Right so god wol youre highnesse iustifie. 659

(95)

Euery day oons showe y*our* high presence 660
Before the Comyn people opynly,
To thentente that ye may yeve audience
To al compleintis shewid p*er*fitly,
Yeuyng theim lauful remedy iustly, 664
Defendynge the pore from Extorcioñ,
Withe al y*our* power / myght & tuicion. 666

Show your-self once a day to your subjects.

(96)

Oure nature desirith to haue a man 667
To reigne here vppon vs w*ith* gou*er*nance,

[1] MS. benet.

ASHBY.   F

Circumspecte of tymes than & whan
He shal execute thyng in assurance,
Quykly & iustly to goddys plesance,   671
Not as a wreche, Tiraunt ne oppresour,
Nor in subtel wiles a Coniectour.   673

(97)

Grounds for going to war.

I wold fain ye wolde kepe in remembrance   674
To be right wele aduised by goode sadnesse,
By discrete prudence & feithful constance
[¹ MS. a any] Er ye begynne werre for any¹ richesse,
Or of fantesie or of symplenesse.   678
For werre may be lightly commensed,
Doubt is how it shal be recompensed.   680

(98)

I mene nat for vnthrifty Cowardise,   681
Whiche is in al Realmes abhominable,
But of wilfulnesse people to supprise,
That micht otherwise be recouerable,
By iuste meanes to god acceptab[l]e,   685
For man knowith nat what he bygynneth,
Howe fortume of vntrifty werre endith.   687

(99)

Seven curses.

Wo worthe debate that never may have peas.   688
Wo worthe penance that askithe no pite.
Wo worthe vengence that mercy may nat sease.
Wo worthe that Iugement that hathe none equite.
Wo worthe that trouthe that hathe no charite.   692
Wo worthe that Iuge that wol no gilte save.
Wo worthe that right that may no favour haue.

Do unto others as you would be done by.

*Facias aliis quod tibi vis fieri & non facias aliis
Quod tibi non vis fieri; hec Socrates.*

(100)

If forgoten be al lawe positife   695
Remembre the noble lawe of nature,
Obse[r]uyng it / al daies of your lif,
And ye shal kepe equite iust & suer,
As to ministre to iche Creature   699

Suche misericorde, iustice & eke grace,
As ye wold be doon to in semblable case. 701

(101)

What is, wisdam, no to be this day wise, 702 Wisdom.
And for to be a fole a nother day,
But euermore to a bide in wise guise
In wordes & dedis to goddes pay.
And in al thing that men wol hym assay, 706
Neither in malice, ne in Cruelte,
Nor owte of tempre for aduersite. 708

(102)

On al wise if your counsail aduise you 709 The Council.
To do thing for your profit and honnour,
Yet heere þair reason & cause why & how,
Thei be to you suche a Solicitour,
Nor for mistruste but for better favour. 713
For perauenture, al thyng discussed,
The case bi you may be better trussed. 715

(103)

A mater discussed & wele betyn 716 Importance
of thorough
discussion.
And reasoned by goode discrecioñ,
The sadnesse therof men may owte setten.
In the contrarie men finde decepcion,
Thurgh thaire owne simple intelleccion. 720
For who that many Reasons wol wele here,
May chese the better & with hym it bere. 722

(104)

Amonges other I wolde you aduertise 723
To be wele aduised in your grauntyng Grants of
offices or
fees.
Any fee or office in any wise
That it securly[1] stande withoute resumyng.
Suche variance hathe be grete rebukyng 727
To many folk, that haue be preferred,
·And aftur of their livelode differred. 729

(105)

A man to be preferred to honour 730 Resumption
of grants
dangerous.
Of fee or office to his grete makyng,
And aftur to be put to dishonnour

[1] MS. serurly.

By resumyng of graunt or forsakyng,
Better had be neu*er* be suche takyng.   734
  It is nought a man to be cherisshed,
  And aftur for pov*er*tee perisshed.   736

(106)

Your serv-
ants' good
opinion. Studie how ye may stande in ful conceite   737
  Of youre owne seruant*es* beneuolence,
Bothe in love & in drede w*ith*oute deceite,
  That thei may haue comfort of yo*ur* pr*e*sence,
For yo*ur* manly & wytti diligence,   741
  In Iustly rulyng with circumspeccion
  Bothe high & lowe w*ith* deue direccio͠n.   743

(107)

Than yo*ur* seruaunt*es* wol bere oute yo*ur* fame,   744
  That in this world It shal nat quenched be,
And reno*w*ne yo*ur* glorious & goode name,
  Spryngyng it for the to eu*er*yche degree,
Blissyng you daily w*ith* goode hert & free,   748
  Whos worship shal be cronicled sadly
  Yn remembryng yo*ur* goode workes gladly.   750

(108)

Virtue not its
own reward. Looke þat your maters be w*ith* god standyng, 751
  And ye shal acheue / yo*ur* blessed entent,
The contrarye shal mischeue in al thing.
  He endith not wele that vngodly ment,
W*ith*oute a reconsiled amendment.   755
  A man of goode wille shal determyne wele,
  A malicious man evel shal fele.   757

(109)

How to listen
to tales. Whan any man maketh suggestion   758
  A yenst another for any greuance
Heerithe hym wele & make sad question
  How his tale may be had in assurance.
But yeueth therto no trusty affiance,   762
  Vntil tyme that ye haue herde the tother.
  Thaugh it seme sothe / it may be founde other.

(110)

Danger of
light cre-
dence. Light credence hath done muche harme & damage 765
  In this world, and eu*er* more herafter shall,

While men wol bileue wilde folk & sauage
  Withoute examynyng lytil or smalle.
  Many men haue had / therby a grete fal,   769
    He that is warned is not deceiued ;
    Yeue no credence / til trouthe be perceiued. 771

(111)

If I shal speke of the vniuersal   772 The common weal.
  And the comyn wele of this Regioñ,
I wol aduise you in especial
  To haue goode guidyng & Inspeccion
  To euery trouble in this nacion,   776
    For thaugh by a litil it begynnyth,
    It may distroy vs al or it endithe.   778

(112)

My lorde, if any man hathe offended   779
  And is brought to the lawe at your owne wille,
Of what maner bloode he be discended,
  Thaugh ye be above & high on the hille,
  Yet lete not people vtterly spille,   783
    If any gracious misericord
    Wol helpe & it to god & man accord. 785

(113)

I mene not / this mercy generally,   786 Use of mercy.
  But to suche people that by lyckelyhede
Bene wele disposed vniuersally,
  To goode gouernaunce & vertuous dede.
  If it be so, ye may deserue grete mede, 790
    This I commyt / to youre discreccioñ,
    As the case askith in submissioñ. 792

Inferas cito penam malefactoribus terre ex quo tibi
constiterit de delictis (illegible) *impediet regnum*
tuum, decapita eum publice vt alii terreantur ;[1]
hec Hermes.

(114)

And if thoffence touche the subuercion   793 Proceed sharply with treason.
  Of the Realme, puttyng it in disturbance,
Procede sharply to deue execucion
  Aftur lawful and rightful ordynaunce,
  In eschewynge al suche mysgouernaunce. 797

[1] MS. terrenant.

For in suche case mercy is nat nedefull,

Neither for the Realme, ne for you spedeful. 799

(115)

Truste me verely, & take it for trouthe,   800

That ye shul moe people hertis conquere

Bi compassion & piteuous routhe

Accordyng to god and his moder dere,

Than bi crueltee, & rigoroussete.   804

So lawe & mercy must be discerned,

That it be suer to god concerned.   806

(116)

The Trea-
surer should
not be a lord. My lorde, lete neuer temporal Lorde   807

Be *your* tresourer, ne *your* Receyvour,

For a meane *per*sonne wol therto accorde

More mete & a bitter (*sic*) solicitour,

More availeable in actiffe socour.   811

For a lordis rewarde is infinite,

A mene *per*sonne may be content *with* lite.[1]

(117)

Choice of
Council. Loke that youre counseil be rather godly set,   814

Wele aged, of goode disposicion,

Than worldly witty & no vertue knet.[2]

Vicious men yeve no gladly inicion

To gracious werke ne goode direccion,   818

But often theire *pur*pose & their entente

Comyn to nought when they be euil ment.   820

*In deum statuas principia tuor*um *negocior*um &

*fines ; hec Gregori*us.

(118)

Take this for gen*er*al conclusion,   821

General con-
clusion. In eue*r*y case where counsail is lackyñg

Committ you to godd*es* direcciõn,

And *your* matiers shall haue goode begynnyng,

And consequently come to goode endyng.   825

For that thyng that is bi god comenced

Shal fynyssh wele *with* hym so insenced.   827

Cum inceperis aliquid bene operare incipias deum

*rogare q*uod *tibi bene succedat ; hec pitagoras.*

[1] Little.   [2] Quaere.

(119)

In al your maters, er ye bygynne, 828 *Think at the beginning what will be the end.*
Thenke what ende wol be the conclusion.
In suche guidyng ye shal grete prudence wynne,
And eschewe mischife & confusion,
In wise forsight & goode discussion, 832
In althing take god at your commencement,
And al thing shal folowe after your intent. 834

(120)

Be wele ware that ye haue not by wisshes, 835 *Good intentions alone are not enough.*
Wisshing that ye had doon or lefte suche thing,
Suche maner reule is nat worthe two Russhes,
To haue cause of repenting your doyiug.
Therfore in iche thing at the begynnyng, 839
Studie sadly by goode discrecion
How ye may take a goode direccioñ. 841

Aspectus ostendit quod iacet in corde plus quam
verbum ; hec Omerus.

(121)

Auoide alwaies frownyng Cowntenaunce 842 *A king's countenance.*
Being fressh, not disguised, ne deyuous,
Ay gladsom and chierful with sad constance,
To the wele of your people amerous,
And þereto with al youre hert desirous, 846
Attempryng you als betwyx colde & fire,
Kepyng your selfe from Angre, wrathe & Ire.

(122)

Retoriq̄ & musyk been two scoles, 849 *Moderation in rhetoric and music.*
Right miche commendable in their nature,
Without restreint many may be fooles
That rekke not to take herin goode mesure.
Neither of thise withoute reule wol be seure, 853
Musyke is disposed to grete lightnesse,
Feire speche for the most parte to grete falsenesse.

(123)

Feire speche I mene i-peynted withoute trouthe, 856
With flatering speche to blere a man is Ie,
Suche personnes to cherisshe it were routhe,
For grete parte of their langage þei do lye

So craftily that is harde theim tespie.   860
　Feire speche mesurably & godly ment,
Accordith to goddis commaundement.   862

(124)

Whan ye be in doubte of any Reulyng,   863
　For to say, do, commaunde or determyn,
Better is of al thise to make cesing,
　Vntil time that god you illumine.
Of al the certente bi wisedam fine,   867
　Thus[1] ye may obserue goode auisement,
And the more suerly topteine youre entent.   869

(125)

Put no ful truste in the Comonalte,   870
　Thai be euer wauering in variance,
But in god feithfulnesses and equite,
　In plaine trouthe, Iustice & goode gouernaunce,
Men haue be bigiled in affiance,   874
　For al other truste is decepcion,
Brynging men to a false conclusion.   876

(126)

Loke that ye kepe alway attemperance   877
　In youre langage & eke commaundement,
Auoidyng al vengeance & displesance
　With al mansuetude[2] conuenient,
This is to your estate expedient.   881
　So the mekenesse in your hert may habonde
To the people of god & of your londe.   883

(127)

I biseche almyghti god of his grace   884
　To sende you longe lif with prosperite,
Hertly comfort, reioysyng & solace,
　And in al your daies tranquillite.
Yet think ther is no suche feli[ci]te,   888
　But al is transitorie and passyng,
Sauf your vertues & godly menyng,   890

(128)

Whiche bene enchaunced[3] in Erthe & also   891
　In heven lastyngly glorified.

　　　[1] MS. This.　　[2] gentleness.　　[3] See 55/284, 58/339.

To your noble blode grete whorship þereto
   Where no Ioy may be now certified,
   Than in thise wise to be sanctified,   895
      For vertu shalbe lauded & preised,
      And misreule atte laste disobeied.   897

(129)

Saint petur saithe þat soubgettes shold be   898   1 Pet. ii. 18.
   Buxom[1] to thar lorde, goode or vnworthy,
Right so a lord shold be in equite,   A lord should deal justly by low folk as weil as high.
   Be-tuyx the high & the lowe Rightfully
   Procedyng & in iche case equally,   902
      Hauyng no respecte to grete alliance,
      Ner therfore dredyng manne-is displeasance.   904

(130)

Whan al lawe, Reason and discrecion,   905   When human powers fail, trust God.
   Wisdam, prudence, counseil & secretnesse
Faile & dispeire / in ymaginacion,
   Than ther may be noon other stabilnesse.
   But trustyng to god & his feithfulnesse   909
      There is verrey relief and goode seurte.
      Sith it is so, lete vs to hym trewe be.   911

(131)

Thinges past, remembre & wele dcuide ;   912   Remember the past ; manage the present ; provide for the future.
   Thinges present, considre & wele governe ;
For thinges commyng, prudently provide ;
   Al thinges in his tyme peise & discerne,
   That to trouthe & worship it may concerne,   916
      Avoidyng from you al Impediment,
      Showing ayenst al vertuous entente.   918

[1] obedient.

III. Dicta & opiniones diversorum philosophorum.

Non exponas te ad dormiend*um* donec consideres oper*a* que fecisti eadem die vt scias si errasti, et in quo, et si feceris quod no*n* debuisti, et si inuen*er*is quod male feceris, tristeris, et si q*uo*d bene leteris et p*er* hoc p*er*uenies q*uo*d sis circa deu*m*; h*ec* Aristotile*s*.

(1)

Before you go to bed, examine your day's be-haviour.

Euery day before ye go to youre bede,   1
  Serche wele al youre quidyng[1] by remembrance.
Yf it be Il, pray god of better spede,
  Yf it be goode, to god be the plesance.
Thus ye may knowe yo*ur* selfe in assurance,   5
  How ye stande w*ith* god and w*ith* his goode grace.
  And daily better you while ye haue space.   7

Rex iustus bene regit. Rex faciens re(c)tu*m* & seruans iusticia*m* regit volunt[at]es pop*u*li et ille qui facit iniusticia*m* & Violenciam regimen illius querit alius qui regnet pro eo. Oportet d*omin*u*m rectificare prius seip*s*um quam pop*u*lum suu*m*; h*ec* Zelon.

(2)

Trust not only in men, but in God.

Truste nat oonly in men is multitude,   8
  Ne in thair myg*h*t, ne in Comon clamour,
But in god & in goode consuetude
  Of trewe iustice, w*ith*out any rigour,
Otherwise than god wolde, owre Saueour: 12
  A Kynge, Reulyng al thynges rightfully
  With lawe reigneth w*ith* al folk plesantly.   14

---

[1] guiding.

Decet Rem agere de nocte cogitare in bono regimine
et in die perficere cognatum; et qui seruos habet seu
subiectos & eos bene gubernat hunc super tuam miliciam
statue principem, et qui hereditates possidet et eas de-
center procurat super prouenientibus tuis ipsum pro-
cu[ra]torem constituas; hec Plato.

(3)

Bethink in the nyght of goode ordennance,　　　15　At night,
　　And in the day execute thy thynkyng.　　　　　plan.
And suche folk as be in goode gouernance,　　　　By day, carry
　　Lete theim bene aboute you awaytyng;　　　　it out.
　　And suche folk as mysreule theire spendyng,　19
　　　Exile theim and other in heritage,
　　　Rulyng wele, take theim for wytty & sage.　21

Iusti nullum timent; qui heret iusticie non habet
vnde aliquem v[er]eatur; quare dixerunt aliqui quod
iusti non habent ex quo deum non formident ex quo
quod Imita[n]tur et suo obediunt mandato. Et si Rex
iustus non est, non est Rex sed predo & violens
spoliatur; hec Aristoteles.

(4)

Yf ye live aftur god & righfull lawe,　　　　　22　If you live
　　Iustly, truly, after goode gouernance,　　　　justly,
Be not in drede ner in no man is awe,　　　　　fear no one.
　　For god hathe constitute an ordennance.
　　Yf man showe in his lif a grete substance,　26
　　　Of his werke being goode & vertuous,
　　　Drede nat al othre þereto odious.　　　28

Gubernare populum non conuenit puero, nec ei qui
est mundanorum negociorum ignarus, nec suam inmu-
tanti concupiscenciam, nec ei qui plurimum vincere con-
cupiscit. Non est differencia inter pue[ro]rum etate &
pue[ro]rum moribus, quia mores hominum non pendent
ex tempore, sed ex eo quod in suis actibus concupiscencias muta[n]tur. Qui concupiscencias vbi quum quan-
tum et vt conuenit, non mutatur bonus ad gubernandum
existit; hec Aristoteles.

(5)

Age is no
proof of
discretion.

Thage of man preuith not discrecion̄,   29
     Ner the youthe of man shewith not madnesse,
Of thise two ye may take inspeccion̄ :
     Whiche guidith hym wisely / with goode sadnesse,
     He is the verray man of Stedfastnesse ;   33
          For that man that childly hym gouernet͡h
          Is a childe, while he that reule obserueth.   35

(6)

A childish
man is not
fit to rule.

So he that hethe childis condicion̄   36
     Ys not acceptable to gouernaunce.
For he that aught to haue subjeccion̄
     Of the people and verrey obeissaunce
     Must put hym selfe in witty assuraunce.   40
          As ye may oft see bi experience,
          He that shal reule must hau grete diligence.   42

Recorderis semper anime tue ut stet in nobili cogitatu.
Pauci enim sunt allegantes aduersus hunc sublimem
statum ; hec Pitagoras.

(7)

Set your
mind on
noble
thoughts.

Lete you[r] mynde be euer in noble thought͡,   43
     In blessid menyng of goode gouernance,
With al other vertues of god sought ;
     Than ye shal acheue al in assurance ;
     Otherwise your werkys gone to mischanche.   47
          Al thyngis begonne wele & godly ment
          Comyn to goode ende withoute repent.   49

Cauete ab eis qui non gubernant se veritate, sed
tamen audiunt eam & non operantur per illam. Et non
paretis Laqueos vt noceatis hominibus nec conemini ad
dampnificandum eos nam ista est res que non abscon-
detur que licet non cognoscatur a principio cognoscetur
finaliter ; hec Hermes.

(8)

Beware of
evil livers.

Beware of theim that lyve not truly,   50
     In iuste gouernance & operacion̄ ;
And noyes no man ne hurte hym wilfully ;

For thaugh ther be no demonstracion
At begynnyng by nominacion,   54
   The ende shall showe euery thinge as it is,   *The end shows what*
   Truly iustly, or els falsly iwys.   56   *everything is.*

Infelix in hoc mundo & malus[1] est qui caret sensu
Sapiencia & doctrina; hec Hermes.

(9)

He may be clept wele an vnhappy man   57   *A man without wit and*
   That is[2] withouten wytte, wisdam and doctrine,   *teaching is unhappy.*
Withoute whiche no personne wele guide hym cañ.
   Therfore euery man aught to do his peine,
   The saide vertues to hau and opteine,   61
    Principally suche as hau gouernance
    To kepe theim selfe & other from greuance.   63

Conuenit vt honores quemlibet iuxta condicionem
suam & ipsius discrecionem et iuxta sui scienciam pub-
licando honorem quem feceris ei vt populo manifesten-
tur bona merentes; hec Hermes.

(10)

Eueri personne, cherissh ye & honoure   64   *Honour every one as he*
   Aftur his merite & discrecion,   *deserves.*
Publisshing to his connyng your fauour,
   Causyng other to take direccion
   To goode & blissed disposicion,   68
    Coraging al people to take grete hede
    To guide theim wele, & to vertue theim lede.   70

Honoranti fit honor.   Aristoteles.

(11)

Worship euery man in his degre,   71   *Honour every man in his*
   Lordis, knyghtes, Squiers and other men,   *degree.*
Some for thair goodnesse & benignite,
   Some for manhode that men of them telleñ,
   Some for grete wisdam that ye in theim sene;   75
    So it shal rebounde to youre honour,
    Causynge you to stande in men-is favour.   77

---

[1] MS. malio.   [2] MS. it.

Non infligas incontinente penam pecc*a*tori s*ed* inter-
mittas[1] spaciu*m* ad exculpand*um* : h*ec* Hermes.

(12)

Don't be too
hasty to
punish.

Set you neuer to hasty to corre[c]te,　　　　　　　78
　　Or punnissh a-noon eueri trespasso*ur*,
But w*ith* leisour theim do protecte,
　　Til ye haue of the trouthe bett*er* savour.
　　Then ye p*ro*cede aft*er* the clamour　　　　　82
　　　　Iustly, truly as the case requirethe,
　　　　Punisshyng hym that falsely conspireth.　　84

Quando rex non potest exprim*ere* suas cupiditates,
qualit*er* potest cupiditates r*e*p*r*imere alior*um* ; et qu*i*
non potest suos defectus p*ro*p*ri*os reprimere no*n* pot*er*it
suum reprimere pop*ulu*m a se distantes.　Ergo decet
Regem incip*er*e do*mi*nare sibi deinde intend*er*e d*o*mi*n*io
alior*um* ; h*ec* Hermes.

(13)

You can't
stop covet-
ousne<del>ss</del> in
others, unless
you suppress
it first in
yourself.

Howe shold a kynge that can nat wel represse　　85
　　His owne couetise, in his owne p*er*sone,
Other men is couetise suppresse,
　　That ben many, and selfe but a-lone.
　　Yef ye wol remedie this mater sone,　　　　89
　　　　Ye must pure youre selfe fyrst w*ith*oute blame,
　　　　And than procede to youre glorious fame.　91

Te non rectificato prius tuu*m* pop*u*lum rectificare non
potes, nec gubernare ip*su*m poteris te errante, / nam
qualit*er* poterit cecus aliu*m* ducere paup*er* ditare aliu*m*,
Inhonoratus seu honore carens aliquem honorabit &
debilis qualit*er* poterit suis virib*us* debilem confortare ?
Certe numqu*am* poterit aliq*u*is alios dirigere[2] nisi qui
sciat & dirigat principalit*er* seip*su*m.　Igitur si im-
mundicias alior*um* volueris abstergere primo cor tuu*m*
illis abstergas eo q*u*od a*n*ima tua exi*st*ente inmunda,
non pot*er*is alium expiare nisi agere velis vt medic*us*
qui a morbo quo p*er*iuntur curare nititur aliu*m*, et seip-
*su*m ab eodem curare non potest ; h*ec* Ar*ist*otel*es*.

[1] MS. intermittere.　　　　[2] MS. diligere.

(14)

A principale note / and directioñ   92
   To gouerne youre soubgettis,
To euery vice making obieccion,
    Looke that the same be not in you, Iwis,
    How may youre self correcte that is amys,   96
      And the same be founde in your personne ?
      Reule youre selfe first and than al other sone.   98

If you want to check vice in subjects, see that you've none yourself.

In vetendo vt non debet dominio Inuidia oritur.
Inuidia mendacium prouenit, mendacio odium, odio,
vero, iniusticia nascitur, iniusticia, inimicicia erumpit,
inimicicia bellum, bello lex perit, et heredita[tes] perduntur et in vetendo vt debetur vero dominio veritas
procreatur, veritate procedit iusticia et iusticia amor
pululatur. Amore[1] vero dona procedunt et tutela cum
quibus lex manutenetur et mundus populis adaugetur.
Aristoteles.

(15)

A prince to misuse his owne Auctorite,   99
   Grete inconueniencis sewe[2] therbi,
Grete mischeif et (*sic*) muche enormite,
    Many recuperable treuly.
    He that vsith his power Rightfully,   103
      Shal prospeire in his vertuous levyng,
      To his famous honnour & grete preisyng.   105

The just Ruler shall prosper.

Quomodo adquiruntur amici ? honorando eos cum
presentes fuerint & benefaciendo eis & commendando
eos cum fuerint absentes ; hec Zelon.

(16)

By thre meanes ye may Freindes purchase :   106
   Firste, when they be present, do theim honour ;
And do wele vnto theim in euery case ;
    When thei be absent, prayse theim with fauour.
    This ye aught to do your peine & labour,   110
      The higher that ye be in high estate,
      Obserue ye this if ye be fortunate.   112

Three ways to get Friends.

---

[1] MS. Amor.   [2] ensue, follow.

Qui est bonor*um* mor*um*, est bone vite & secure, & ho*min*es diligunt eu*m*; et qui est malor*um* mor*um*, est male vite, & fugiu*n*t eu*m* ho*min*es; h*ec* Socrates.

(17)

All folk love well-mannerd people.

Wele manered people bene of goode lif,   113
   And al folk theim loven for thair goodenesse.
Euel named bene often in striff,
   And men fle theim for thair vnthriftynesse.
     Thus ye may eschewe many a distresse   117
       Taccompaignie you with folk vertuous,
       And avoide from you people vicious.   119

Qui d*omi*natu*r* ho*min*i*bus* *necesse* h*a*b*et* h*a*b*e*re me-mori*am* semp*er* triu*m*. Primu*m* est gentis plurime que subest ei. S*ecundum* est q*uia* licet sint sub suo d*omi*nio liberi su*n*t & no*n* serui. Tertiu*m* est q*uod* sua d*omi*nacio durare no*n* potest nisi modico te*m*por*e*; h*ec* Hermes.

(18)

Three things for a lord to bear in mind.

A lorde aught to hau thre thinges in mynde,   120
   First, nu*m*bre of folk in his governance.
Seconde, that they be free, nat bonde in kynde.
   The thirde that he hathe no sad assurance
   Of his lordeship in longe contynuance.   124
     So ye may Reuolue in cogitacion
     That here ther is no longe habitacion̄.   126

Sciat*is* q*uod* p*opulus* obedit benefacienti sibi, nec potest accidere Regno bene nisi q*uu*m benefacias p*opu*lo; nam q*uum* populus[1] carebit eo erit d*omi*nus sui t*ame*n; h*ec* Hermes.

(19)

Folk obey those who do them good.

The people haue a goode condicion,   127
   To yeue to theire goode doer obesance;
Take this for a trewe erudicion,
   The roiaulme may neu*er* be in assurance,
   Bot folk bene wele doon-to w*ith*out distance.   131
     Kepe theim laufully in peas & in rest,
     This[2] they shall obey youre highnesse most best.

---

[1] MS. d*omi*nus; but the English version runs, "For when the people is gone, the prince abideth lord of himself alonlie."
[2] This = thus.

Non egrediatur ex ore vestro Indignacionis tempore
verbum turpe, quia hec est Res dehonestans, et ducens
ad penam ; hec Hermes.

(20)

In any tyme of Indignacion,   134   Never use
foul or angry
rebukes.
  Or in other reason of displesance,
Withowte al other excusacion
  Tuche not of fowle rebukynge speche vtterance,
  Nor of no maner vengeable semblance.   138
    But rather attende with mansuetude
    Tamende folk, than to fere[1] with wordes rude. 140

Melius & nobilius in hoc mundo est bona fama & in
alio mundo exclusio a pena. Valencius est tacere quam
loqui cum ignorante & solitudinem querere quam iungere
se malis. Sapiencia adquiritur humilitas bona voluntas
pietas & priuacio peccatorum ; hec Hermes.

(21)

The best thinge in al this wide world is this,   141   A good report
is the best
thing in this
· wide world.
  For to be renouned in blessed fame.
Who wol this haue, must be wytty & wise ;
  By vnthriftynesse, men lesen theire name.
Speke not to folis that bene in diffame ;   145
    Stablisshe you in your hert to grete wisdam,
    Withoute whiche lost may be a grete kyngdam.

Qualis sit sensus ostendit eloquium ; hec logmon.
Et ex habundancia cordis os loquitur ; hec Omerus.
Et os ostendit quod iacet[2] in corde ; hec Socrates.

(22)

To be of to myche speche is a grete vice ;   148   Much talking
is a great
vice.
  To be of to litle speche is Fooleship.
Ches[3] therfore þe best if ye wolbe wise,
  Bestowyng your wordes to your worship
  Truly, wisely longyng to your lordeship.   152
    Suche as people bene, suche is thair vsance,
    After thair hertes þei make thair vttrance.   154

---

[1] frighten.   [2] MS. iacit.   [3] MS. Thes.
ASHBY.   H

Tribus de causis honorant*ur* Reges, ex leg*um* Institu-
ci*one* bonar*um*, ex bonis Regionib*us* co*n*querendis et ex
desertar*um* populacione terrar*um* ; hec Aristotiles.

(23)

A king gains
honour—
1. by good
laws; 2. con-
quering
lands;
3. peopling
deserts.

By thre thing*es* is honnoured a kynge,   155
    Fyrste for makynge of lawe acceptable,
Seconde for many landes conqueryng,
    The thirde to make desertis habitable,
    W*ith* myche people þere to couenable ;   159
        Thus a goode kynge is taken as he is,
        And renounned here, and in heuyn blisse.   161

Opera hominu*m* non ad vnguem discucias, q*ui*a cum
ho*min*es non possu*n*t erroribus om*n*ino excludi si multu*m* examinent*ur* et districte co*n*fundetur tua discrecio ;
igit*ur* a aliquib*us* eor*um* au*er*tendi sunt oculi, ad in-
dulgendu*m* eisdem.   Hiis eni*m* penes te ex*istentibus*
corda dirigent*ur* ip*s*or*um* & procedent ad melius facta
tua.   A*ri*st*ot*el*es.*

(24)

Don't blame
folk too
much.

Blame never people to the vtterest,   162
    Ner never examine thaim to straitly.
W*ith*owte blame or erro*ur* is not the best ;

Forgive
sometimes.

    Soumtyme ye must forgeue graciously,
    And thus ye shall wynne hert*es* stedfastly.   166
        Euery man-is traspasse be not lyke ;
        Considre theim wele as man polletyke.   168

Ignorancia ho*min*is tribu*s* causis cognoscit*ur*.   In
non h*a*bendo cogitatum in rectificaci*one* sui ip*s*ius, &
no*n* repugnando suis cupiditatibus, et gubernando se
co*n*silio sue consortis in eo q*uo*d scit & q*uo*d nescit ;
hec So*c*rat*es.*

(25)

A man's
ignorance is
shown by—
1. not cor-
recting him-
self; 2. not
hating covet-
ousness ;
3. following
his wife's
advice.

By thre thing*es* a man-is ignorance   169
    Ys knowen, hymselfe not rectifie,
To couetise to haue no repugnance,
    Bi his wiffe his counseil hym to fortifie :
    Thise thre thing*es* no man may Iustifie.   173
        Therfore take goode hede and sad attendance
        To eschewe the mischeif of this dance.   175

Decet regem cognoscere adherentes sibi .quorum
quemlibet statuat suo loco iuxta cuiuscumque discrecionem Sapienciam et felicitatem, prouidens vnicuique
iuxta exigenciam meritorum; nec sint talia dona que
non acceptentur nec placeant; hec Hermes.

(26)

A kynge sholde knowe al his owne seruantes,   176   A king must know his servants,
  Their rule, ther gidyng and condicion ;
And to eueriche of theim make his grauntes,   and reward them according to their deserts.
  Afteir their wisdam & discrecion
  To their merites make prouision,   180
    In eueryche degree mete to their desert ;
    Acceptable & plesant in thair hert.   182

Hillaritas est intelligendum signum & e contra; hec
Hermes.

(27)

To dissimile, sum men holde a wisedam,   183   Don't dissimulate, except under necessity.
  And it may be in some herd distresse,
But for the moste in euery kyngdam,
  Suche as ye be by your chere expresse,
  Either in hate or in loue showe thexcesse.   187
    And so men shall knowe you bi countenaunce
    How men shall guide theimself to your plesance.

Decet hominem non odire nec offendere illum qui
eum offendit; immo bene faciat & mitiget motus &
verba eius; hec hermes.

(28)

If your servauntes displea (sic) your highnesse,   190   If folk displease you,
  As euery man is nat in that seurte
To guide hym perfitely in stedfastnesse,
  Yet showe hym louely your benygnite   be gracious to them.
  Withoute hatefull wrathe of your dignite.   194
    A Soubget may nat bere your displeasance
    But your grace be showed to your grevaunce. 196

Quando errabit amicus penes te non recedas ab eius
amicicia donec remaneat ad in eo quo (sic) ipsum videris
posse Rectificari; hec Aristoteles.

(29)

If a friend
offends you,

If ye haue any friende in your Favour,   197
　Thaugh he erre or do to you displeasance,

don't make
too much
fuss about it.

Make not of his defaute to meche clamour
　While he hathe any power or substance
　　To rectifie his defaute or greuance,   201
　　　Puttyng hym in his aquital & peyne
　　　To aveange hym, ye muste your self refreyne. 203

Rex sapiens imperat cum mansuetudine & placabili-
tate; quod non imperat displicitate & superbia &
perpere[1] cum bonis propter illud quod putat facere
iusticiam rectam et equam; hec hermes.

(30)

Be meek and
kind to all.

Obserue mekenesse in youre maundement   204
　With al benignite and mansuetude,
Takyng this goode blessid aduertisment,
　Neuer in displesant consuetude,

Don't use
rude words
to good folk.

Ne with rigorous wordes, ne with rude,   208
　Yeue no charge ayenst goode people, namely
　While ye wot Iustifie theim equally.   210

Si Rex aggregavit thesaurum & non expenderit illum
vbi conuenerit, aut perdet illum aut Regnum; hec hermes.

(31)

Unless you
spend your
treasure well,

If ye make of tresour aggregacion̄   211
　By any maner meanes possible,
To youre estate & nominacion̄
　But thexpense therof be incorrigible,
Conuenietly to men visible   215

you'll lose
it or your
realm.

　Bestowed, either loste is the treasour,
　Or elles the Roiaulme bi men is clamour.   217

Duo sunt laudabilia & bona, lex & Sapiencia, quia
lege cohibemur a peccatis et Sapiencia adquiremus
cunctas bonitates; Rex est bonus qui non permittit
vnum alium offendere; hec Aristoteles.

(32)

Law and
Wisdom are
two good
things.

Two thinges be right goode and commendable,   218
　That bene, Lawe & Wisdam in temprance.

[1] MS. *proprie.*

Lawe constreineth folk from offence culpable,
  And wisdam guideth al goode assurance.
Al thise two thynges kepith in substance,   222
  And rectifie iche man in his degree,
  That noon hurt oþer by Iniquite.   224

Non rideas multum, nec irasceris, quia ista sunt duo
opera fatuitatis. Aristoteles.

(33)

Two thinges bene signe of grete foleshiꝑ,   225   *Too much laughing and too much wrath are signs of Folly.*
  The toon is laugh myche in compaigni
The tother is to wax wrothe in shenship,
  Thise two bene the vices of grete folie
Causyng many other to multiplie.   229
    Therfore guide your selfe in suche blessednesse
    That the people may Ioy of your highnesse. 231

Decet Regem ad sua seruicia sucepere quem prius-
quam regnaret bonum et fidelem cognouit. Cum Rex
postquam regnauerit non valet eos bene cognoscere quia
omnes ei postmodum adulantur & honorantur eundem ;
hec Socrates.   (34)

A kynge sholde take of his olde acquaintance,   232   *A king should employ old servants whom he proved before he reigned.*
  His familier seruauntes vertuous,
That he knewe before his Regne of Substance,
  Wele disposed, trewe, not malicious.
When he reigneth, eche man wolbe Ioyous   236
  To glose hym, to please hym with al circumstance :
  Harde it were to knowe than their variance.   238

Qui reputat omnes Homines equaliter, Amicos habere
non potest ; hec Socrates.

(35)

Oon thing I wolde aduertise your hignesse,   239   *Don't think every man is the same, (some are wise; some, fools ;) or you'll have no true friends.*
  Take not euery mañ in oon qualite :
Oon is wise and a nother in lewdenesse,
  Sum be in welth, sum in aduersite,
Sum be mery and sum in nycyte ;[1]   [1 folly] 243
  Who that cannat disseure wise from bad
  Shal haue no verrey freendes þat be sad.   245

Qui gubernat bene seip*s*um, expedit e*ss*e gube*r*nator;
h*ec* Plato.

(36)

A good
Governor is
he who can
rule himself.

In this wise ye shul knowe a gouernour   246
    Hable to reule & guide in euery place,
That can be in hym self a goode myrrour,
    Guidynge hym selfe aftur oure lord*es* grace,
    Shewyng euer a playne & a trewe face.   250
        He that can not his owne p*er*sonne goue*r*ne,
        How shuld he other folk*es* therin lerne?   252

Tri*b*us de causis dolet homo, de diuite qui venit ad
paup*er*tatem, de honorabili qui dispeccionem incurrit,
& de sapiente que*m* ignorans derisit; hec Plato.

(37)

Three things
to grieve a
man.

Of thre thinges a man may be heuy :   253
    Riche man for to come to pouerte;   (1)
A worshipful man in dispite reuly;[1]   (2)
A wiseman,[2] of the ignorant to be   (3)
    Scorned or mocked, þat folk may it se.   257
        So this world is not certeine ne stable,
        But whirlyng a bowte and mutable.   259

Non expectes me*r*entib*us* benefacere quousq*ue* requi-
rat illud, s*ed* eis ben*e*facias a tempo*re*; h*ec* Plato.

(38)

If a man has
deservd re-
ward, give
it him at
once, before
he asks for it.

If any man haue deserued rewarde   260
    For his meritis & goode goue*r*nance,
In his hasty recompense be toward,
    Competently betyme by yo*ur* puissance,
    Er it be askad w*ith*oute daleance,   264
        And by yo*ur* selfe lete it be doon frely :
        That shal be best, and the more price sette by. 266

Non irasceris subito, q*uia* si facere consueue*r*is do-
*m*inabit*ur* tibi Ira.   Cum posse ha*b*es vites Iram q*ue*
no*n* p*er*mittet rei inspicere finem; h*ec* Plato.

(39)

Don't get
angry sud-
denly.

I counseil, be nat sodenly wrathfull :   267
    And ye be accustomed so to do,
And ofte displeased & also Ireful,

        [1] ruefully.   [2] MS. A wiseman man.

It shal ou*er*come you when ye wold nat so,
That ye may not tempre you*r* self therfro.   271

   Therfore guide youreself in suche pacience,   *Be patient.*
   That wrath ou*er*come you nat for negligence.   273

Si volueris scire natura*m* alicui*us* sup*er* aliq*uo*, co*n*-
sulas eu*m*, et ex hoc cognosces sua*m* *in*iq*u*itate*m* vel
equitate*m*, & sua*m* bon**ī**tate*m* vel maliciam ; h*ec* Plato.

(40)

Yef ye wol knowe euery man is nature,   274   *To know a*
   Wit, purpos, entente and condicion,   *man's nature,*
                                                                   consult him
Counseil w*it*h hym of sum thyng in grete Cure ;   *on a matter of import-ance.*
   Anoon ye shall knowe his entencion
   Of goode or Il his disposici**õ**,   278
      And whether he be set to equite,
      Or ellis to false iniquite.   280

Scias q*uo*d int*er* dei dona, Sapiencia excellencior est.
Dilige sapiencia*m*, et audias sapientes, et obedias deo ;
h*ec* Plato.

(41)

Of al the yef*tes* that eu*er* god made   281   *Wisdom is the best gift*
   Wisedam is the most excellent by name,   *that God made.*
By whiche vertue wol encrece and not fade,
   And most is enchaunced worship & fame,
   And most eschew*it*h vices & eke blame,   285
      And bryngith a man best to godd*es* plesance,
      And kepith best in worldly assurance.   287

Adu*er*sariu*m* tuu*m* contra te machinantem, nitaris ad
equita[te]m reducere, pocius qu*am* *pro*curare vindicta*m ;*
nam vindicta est utriq*ue* da*m*pnosa, & *pre*seruans equi-
tas vtilis est vtriq*ue ;* h*ec* Plato.

(42)

Be neuer disposed to grete vengeance,   288   *Don't long for Venge-*
   Yf ye may other wise do by Iustice,   *ance.*
But entrete folkes to obedience,
   By meke & gentil word*es* in feir guise.   *Win folk by gentleness.*
   Thus men shalbe wonnen to you*r* seruice.   292
      Vengeance is nat often prophitable,
      But the contrary is commendable.   294

Reduc homines ad equitatem suauiter; al[i]oquin
eris in labore & pugna cum eis; hec Plato.

(43)

Use gentle-
ness first;

Reduce your subgettes to equite,   295
    Firste swetely and by meanes Resonable ;
Yf thei wol rest in their iniquite,

then, force.

    Compelle theim bi vigour couenable,
Fyghtyng a-yenst theim til they be stable,   299
     Kepyng your self ever in trewe iustice,
     And doubte not your entente thei shal accomplissh.

Qui non mansuescit vel acquiescit castigacione blanda,
fac eum mansuefieri correpcione turpi vel aspera ; hec
Hermes.

(44)

If a man
won't yield
to persua-
sion, punish
him sharply.

Yf ye can not brynge a man by mekenesse,   302
    By swete glosyng wordes and feire langage,
To the entente of your noble highnesse,
    Correcte him sharpely with rigorous rage,
To his chastysment and ferful damage ;   306
     For who that wol nat be feire entre[te]d,
     Must be foule & rigorously threted.   308

Noli seruiri ab aliquo de eo quod non est a natura
sibi licet debite teneatur, quia plurimum tecum turba-
bitur, cum labor[ar]e oporteat in faciendo eo ad quod
non est aptus ; hec Plato.

(45)

Let folk
serve you
according to
their nature.

Considre ye euery man-is nature,   309
    A[nd] aftur their oune disposicion,
Receyve theire seruice & put theim in crure[1] (*sic*),
    Acordyng as shal be expedicion
To bothe parties in admission.   314
     To chose a man nat apte to youre seruice,
     How shold he your ful pleasure to accomplice ?

Non tuearis illum qui per te defendi intendit in eo
per quod tua bonitas minuatur vel minus apprecieris.
Propterea ymmo in aliis rebus promoneas & iuues eundem ; hec Plato.

[1] ? for "cure."

(46)

Protecte ne defende no man by you*r* myght, 316

Don't protect wrong-doers.

  That by you to holpyn antendith,

That shold mynyssh you*r* goodenesse or ellis right,

  For any pite that he pretendith.

Resonable wisedam god you sendeth 320

    To diseure right from wronge prudently ;

    Therfore support never wronge wyttyngly. 322

Modicu*m* no*n* reputes vnu*m* Inimicu*m* habere, q*ui*a malum magis qu*a*m cogites tibi poterit oriri ab eo. Res que est contra natura*m*, vires h*a*bet in suo inicio forciores, et res nat*u*ralis forciores suo fine ; h*e*c Plato.

(47)

Repute neuer oon enemye litel, 323

Never think a foe too small.

  For he may hurt you more bi his malice

Then ye wolde wene þat a wreche & fykel

  Might greve or compasse for to accomp[l]ice.

In-disposed[1] men myche hurt can deuise. 327

    Of youre enemye take goode attendance

    þat he hynde[2] you nat by his greuance. 329

Non est conueniens prauor*um* d*o*m*i*nium, qu*i*a licet bonu*m* videat*ur* aliq*u*o tempo*re*, ad malum *tamen* deuenit finem ; h*e*c Plato.

(48)

Lordeship of Shrewes is nat accordant 330

The rule of Shrews is an evil.

  Ne conuenient to be cherisshed ;

Thaugh at sum tymes it semith plesant,

  Euyl thinge at eend is p*er*isshed,

And comyth to nought & is vanyshed, 334

    Where goo[d]nesse abideth in assurance,

    And evel is reward w*it*h myschance. 336

Magis detrime[n]tum q*uo*d regnum habere potest, est propter elatos corde habentes meliorem qu*am* meruerunt statum ; nam alios se meliores despiciunt, et tali modo ordinacio Regis peruertitur et turbatur; h*e*c Plato.

---

[1] ? a genuine word, or for 'ill-disposed.' See 'wele-disposed,' 67/967, 75/710.   [2] .hinder.

(49)

Pride is the
greatest
harm to a
realm.

Of al the detrimentis, hurtis & hyndrance   337
  That may betide to a Roiaulme, is pride
To be enchaunced to grete gouernance
A-yenst desert, and other put aside.
  The better he wold euer ouer-ride,   341
    And peruerte al the kynges ordenaunce,
    And auenture it in great distourblance.   343

Saluus est qui seruit Regibus in fidelitate, & cum
pietate populo; nec status in quo est decipit eum, nec
propter bonum quod possidet, nec propter malum
aliquatenus desperat quo grauatur; hec Plato.

(50)

He who
shows pity,

He is seure and saufe that seruith kynges,   344
  In fidelite shewyng grete pite
To al people in his doinges.
  His estate shal come to prosperite,
  Whether he be in welthe or aduersite.   348

is lovd every-
where.

    Lerne this lesson, to be right piteuous,
    And ye shul come to loue in euery house.   350

Consulas in negociis equalem tibi, quia ipse maxime
intelligit quod opus est tibi; hec Plato.

(51)

Take counsel
of your
equals.

Aske counseil of a man to you equale,   351
  In your grete nedys and meche besynesse.
He can yeve you best counseil & moost formal;
  He knowethe what longeth to your prowesse,
  To your estate, honnour & noblenesse.   355
    Suche lessons haue otherwhile in mynde,
    In whiche wisdam & profyt ye shul fynde.   357

Moderata verecundia facit hominem omitti quod non
competit sibi; nimis superflua facit omitti quod competit
sibi, sed diminuta et modica, ad quod non competit
cogit incedi; hec Plato.

(52)

Modesty is
helpful.

A moderate shame makith men to leve   358
  Many shameful thinges & vnfyttyng;

Ouer moche shame makith men to bileve

Don't be too shamefast.

  To leve that thing þat were to hym fyttyng.

Goode discrecion take to youre lernyng,   362

  What is to [be] lefte & what to be doon,

  And guide you aftur goode discrecion.   364

Non vtaris operibus cum verba sufficiant; hec Plato.

(53)

Use neuer for to execute in dede,   365

Don't act, when a word is enough.

  Where ye may haue deue execucion

Bi wordes, and al folkes iustly lede.

  What nedith Rigour in submission

  Of hym amendyng his transgression ?   369

    He that may reule wele bi benignite,

    Leue Rigour, or in vnrest shal he be.   371

Res regi prohibita censetur ebrietas. Quia Rex regni
sit custos : quam turpe erit ipsum sui custodia indigere.
Inter Reges est felix ille, in quo dominium predecess-
orum dirigitur ; & infelix est ille, in quo ipsum subsi-
ditur & priuatur ; hec Plato.

(54)

That king is ful blessed & happy   372

The king is happy who doesn't misrule and get drunk.

  That can kepe hym from mysreule & dronkship,

And directe his leuelode profitably,

  Encreasyng his heritage and lordeship.

  What dishonnour is to hym, & shenship,   376

    That mysguideth his liuelode & lesith,[1]

    And al his reuenues mysvseth !   378

Non te intromittas ad aliquid faciendum quousque
sensus prouiderit illud delectabiliter faciendum; hec
Plato. (55)

Neuer entremete you of erthly thinge   379

Don't begin till you've secured a good ending.

  Til your wise wytt haue prouided before

How it may be doon to a goode endyng.

  Than accomplisshe it with hert more & more.

  He that dothe nat soo, is lewde & a poore.   383

    A thing foreseien is light texecute.

    Unauised men, foles bene repute.   385

---

[1] loseth.

Oportet iudicem no*n* rigidu*m* e*s*se sermone co*n*tra
maleficii patratores, q*uia* si no*n* se ha*b*eret hoc mo*d*o
abuteretur auct*ori*tate scensoris ; h*e*c Plato.

(56)

Judges
should not
speak too
savagely to
ill-doers.
A Iuge shold not be in worde rigorous   386
   A-yenst malefactours in eny wise.
He is to þat power contrarious,
  If he any boistorous worde deuise ;
  But in gentil and most piteous guise   390
    He must attempr*e* wele his Iugement,
    That no bousterous Rigo*ur* þe*r*e be ment.   392

Qualis Rex, talis po*pulus*. Cupiditates & hominu*m*
voluntates rep*er*iuntu*r* iux*ta* Regum cupiditates & voluntates ip*sorum* ; h*e*c Plato.

(57)

Like king,
like folk ;
Suche as the kynge is, suche bene al other,   393
  Bothe in wille & also in couetise ;
The toon may not be w*i*t*h*oute the tother ;
  For the kynge hathe the charge theim to supprise,
  That wolde surmonte, or in vices arise.   397
    The kyng may make his people as hym liste,
bad or good.   Either evil or vertuous & iust.   399

Quid e*st* quo cognoscitu*r* iustus ? Ex eo q*uo*d non
agat aliquid da*m*pnosum alicui, nec loq*ui*tur mendaciu*m*
ob sui p*r*ofectu*m* ; h*e*c Plato.

(58)

A just man
harms no
one, and lies
not for gain.
A Iuste man shalbe knowen in this wise,   400
  To do no man Iniuri wilfully,
Ner ly not for his p*r*ofett in suche guise
  That it shuld harme any man skilfully.
Thus eu*er*y man sholde lyve rightfully,   404
    And euer to haue God before his face,
    By the whiche he shal Ioy & blisse p*ur*chase. 406

Si Rex omittit inuest[ig]are po*pu*li sui *facta* milicie
sue & inimico*rum*, non vno die securus de regno suo ;
h*e*c Hermes.

(59)

Yf a king serche nat the condicioñ 407
  Of his people, knyg[t]hode, & enemy,
And al thair dedes bi discrecioñ,
  He may nat be sure of his regne treuly,
  Not oon day, but he attende prudently 411
    With circumspecioñ and gouernance
    To put al thise thinges in assurance. 413

Quam bene e*st* populo, cuius Rex est bone discrec*io*nis
& boni consilii, et sapiens in scienciis ; & qu*a*m male
e*st* ipsi quu*m* ad *eo* pre*d*ictoru*m* deficit ei ! hec Hermes.

(60)

How goode & blissed is that Regioñ 414
  That haue a king wise, discrete, & witty
Bothe in science & circumspectioñ,
  That can guide al his soubgette*s* seurely ;
  And if he be the contrary treuly, 418
    Al gothe at[1] hauoke and mysgouernance,
    And the Roiaulme diuided & in distance. 420

Quando Rex despiciet a*li*qu*id* modicum de quo facere
debet, augebit*ur* illud, sicut debilis infirmitas corp*o*ris,
cui non occurrit*ur* cum medicina, magnificabitur, &
totu*m* corp*us* molestabit ; h*e*c Hermes.

(61)

That king that reputeth that he shold do 421
  For litil or nought, It shal multiplie
As a litil sykenesse dothe in man ; so
  Where first w*ith* litil he might modifie,
  And w*ith* litle labo*ur* it rectifie ; 425
    For of a litle sparkel a grete fyre
    Comyth, displeasaunt to many a sire. 427

Interest regis informare filium scienciis qualit*er* suum
Regnu*m* conser*u*et, et qualit*er* sit rectus in pop*u*lo suo,
et qualit*er* dirigat milicia*m* suam ; nec p*er*mittit eu*m*
multu*m* vti venacione nec aliis vagac[i]o[n]ib*us* ; & in-
struat eum loqui composite, & vitare faciat vanitates ;
*h*ec Hermes.

---

[1] MS. As gothe &. Mr. H. Bradley suggests 'Al gothe at'
as a possible emendation.

Unless a king
finds out his
folks' state,

he can't be
sure of his
reign for a
day.

How blest is
the land that
has a wise
king !

If the king
neglects a
small ill, it
will grow like
disease in a
body.

(62)

A king sholde enfourme his sone in this wise,   428
    With science to conserue his Region,
And to be rightful to folk in goode guise ;
    Knyght-hode to put in goode direccion ;

    To to moche huntyng haue none intencioñ,   432
      Ner to wanderinges, ne to vanite ;
      And to speke ornatly with equite.   434

Interest Regis quod sua beneficia in bonis viris apar-
eant, et in hiis qui scire intuentur[1] vt ob hoc ad predicta
melius mutantur ; hec Hermes.

(63)

It longithe to a king For to auance   435
    And to do wele to goode men & vertuous,
And thei shal wille wele his profitt & assurance ;
    Where misgoverned men and vicious,
    And delicate men and delicious,   439
      Wol tendre thair owne proper volunte,
      Hauyng no regard to other bounte.   441

Interest Regis, cum vult sibi seruiri ab aliquo de suo
ministerio, scire prius mores ipsius & qualiter se gubernet, & domum suam et socios. & si percepit eum esse
bonorum morum, et gubernatorem status sui, & obserua-
torem legis, & tollere[2] pacienter qui contingunt sinistros
euentus, faciat sibi seruiri ; si non, de[te]stetur eum ;
hec Hermes.

(64)

A kynge sholde take seruantes famulere ;   442
    First knowe their maners & thair gouernance,
How thay reulen their howse withoute dere,
    And to thair feliship in assurance,
    Yf thei be wele named in substance,   446
      Wele demeaned, & of lawe a keper,
      Pacient, take thaim for feithful louer.   448

Purum Animum diligentem te dilige, meliorem enim
fratre ex patre et matre optante mortem tuam vt here-
ditet bona tua.   Hec Hermes.

[1] MS. intuitur.   [2] MS. tolleret.

(65)

Yf ye finde a pure freinde, Louyng and sure,   449   Cherish a true Friend
   Constant, wele-willed and beneuolent,
And eke stedfastly a-bide and endure,
   And euer his actes to you wele ment,
   Accordyng to your pleasire and entent,   453
    Do cherissh hym better than your brother,   better than a Brother.
    So that he excelle in loue al other.   455

Qui deficit in eo quod tenetur Creatori suo, quanto
magis deficit in omnibus aliis bonis operibus. Hec
Hermes.

(66)

He that lackythe for to do his duetie   456   He who does not his duty to Jesus,
   To al myghti Iesu, oure creatour,
In al tymes of his necessite,
   And displeasith ofte owre Sauiour,
   Standyng owte of goddes loue & fauour,   460
    Must nedis lakke myche more oþer goode werke,   will lack other good works.
    Wytnessyng hermes, the noble, goode clerke.   462

In multum dormiendo non est profectus sed dampnum. Assuesco igitur benefacere nocte et die, ad hoc
quod medium vite tue in ocium non expendas.

(67)

To slepe miche, is no profytt ne availle,   463   Too much sleep is hurtful.
   But hurte, damage and derogacion.
Therfor, for remedie and acquitaile,
   Accustome you bi goode probacioñ.   Do good constantly,
   For to do wele withoute mutacion,   467
    That the myddyl of your liffe be not spent   so that your life may not be wasted.
    In ydelnesse, ne in vnthrifte myswent.   469

Beatus est ille Rex qui mutat suas leges in melius;
et melior & nobilior est Rex qui in regno suo commutat
legem malam propter bonam; hec Hermes.

(68)

That kynge is blissed and honourable   470   The Im-prover of Laws is blest;
   That chaungeth his lawes for the better,

In goode actes & statutes laudable,

but the
Changer of
Bad to Good
is more
glorious.

By the whiche[1] whiche (*sic*) he is gretter & gretter,

That can of Injury be a letter,[2]   474

Into his glorious fame Renommed,

So often that it may not be sommed.   476

---

(69)

In al your noblay and prosperite,   477

In your worshipful richesse & blessed name,

Keep a good
Conscience
and an un-
blemisht
character.

Kepe ye thre thinges for your moost seurete—

Goode conscience and vnblemysshed fame,

By the whiche ye shul be kepte from grete grame;

And from al dishonour and vice coarted,[3]

And to grete worshiꝑ þere-by exalted.   483

hec Ouidius.

Dic bona de amico tuo cui vis occurrere, eo quod inicium amoris est benedicere, et Inicium odii maledicere; hec Socrates.

(70)

Speak well of
your Friend,
and he'll love
you.

Say goode of your freinde in al freenly wise.   484

The begynnyng of loue is to say wele;

The begynnyng of hate, with evil guise.

Thus man-is tonge shewith swetnesse or felle.[4]

Of al thinges the tonge berith the belle.   488

The tonge breketh boon, thaugh he be tendre,

And shethe[5] many men thaugh he be slendre. 490

Maior rectificacio est dirigere Regem elongare se a malis, ne mala que fiunt imputentur eidem; hec Socrates.

(71)

The best rec-
tification is to
lead a king
from evil.

The most grettest Rectificacion   491

Ys, from evel thinges to directe a kinge,

Leest vnto hym fal Reprobacioñ

By his euil doyng or mysguidyng.

Meche people awayte vppon his reulyng: 495

Yf it be goode, people greetly reioise;

Yf he be euel, for suche thei wol hym noyse. 497

---

[1] ? text corrupt; needs 'But he is the gretter' &c.
[2] hinderer   [3] forced   [4] cruel   [5] shoots (? sleeth, slays).

Rex est uelud est magnus fluuius, nascens de p*ar*uo;
vnde, si dulcis est, dulces sunt omnes p*ar*ui; et si
salsus, omnes erunt salsi; hec Plato.

(72)

The king is a grete and a myghti Floode, 498
 Ascended and comen of many smale.

Yf the floode be swete, douce, fresshe & goode,
 Of suche sauour & Fresshnesse bene the vale.

If it be salte, of suche taste w*ith*oute tale 502
 Bene the tother, by al man*er* nature.
  As the kyng is, suche bene al in his cure. 504

The King is
like a mighty
River.

If he is sweet,
his subjects
are too;

if salt, so are
they.

Non iudices pr*i*usqu*am* vtrosq*ue* audias c*on*tenden-
tes; hec Plato.

(73)

In any striff, make neuer iugement 505
 Til ye haue herde boothe p*ar*ties wisely,
Leest after ye haue cause to repente,
 For lack of Foresight and serching treuly.
A kynges worde muste nedys stand iustly; 509
 Therfore in al thing be wele approved,
  That nought eschape, digne to be reproued. 511

Don't judge
till you've
heard both
sides.

Cum habueris amicu*m*, expedit q*u*od sis suimet Amicus; nec expedit q*u*od sis inimicus inimici ip*s*ius; h*e*c
Plato.

(74)

If ye haue a frende, be frendly to his; 512
 If ye haue an enemy comb*er*ous,
Ye aught nat to be his enemy I-wis,
 But euer in charite vertuous.
Thus ye may betuyxe bothe be Ioyous, 516
 And set youre selfe in quiete & Rest;
  And thus ye may demene you moost surest. 518

Be a friend to
your Friend's
friends; and
don't be a
foe to your
foes.

Si pius es, non cum ea pietate que conuertat*ur* in
da*m*pnu*m*. Et penam merentibus inferre non differas;
et ad roborandam Legem labora, quia in ea domini
timor constat. Ari*s*totel*e*s.

ASHBY.   K

(75)

Don't let your Pity turn into harm.

If ye be disposed to grete pite,   519
    Lete not that into harme be conuerted,
Ner differred peine to theim that worthy be
    To be punisshed in vice peruerted.

The fear of God consists in keeping the Law.

Ner lete nat your lawes be subuerted,   523
    But theim mayntene and sustene rightfully,
    In whiche the drede of god standith iustely.   525

Debiliorem ex inimicis tuis, forciorem te reputas, eo modo requirens tuam miliciam,[1] velud qui ex magnis causis emergentibus egens ad sui tutelam Requirit eandem; hec Aristoteles.

(76)

Think your least Foe stronger than yourself;

Youre leest enemy, Repute ye strenger   526
    Than your selfe in his fals Iniquite,
Suppressyng hym, leest he a-bide lenger
    in his feruein malice and subteltee;
    Puttyng your personne euer in seurte;   530

and keep him under your foot.

    And kepe your enemy vnder your fote;
    To be in rest, þere is noon other boote.   532

Si sapiens Rex fieri volueris, ad Rudos & inscios non auertas, Sed ad illos qui sapiencia te transcendunt; hec Asseron.

(77)

The Wise King must keep clear of Fools,

If a kynge wol be wytty and eke wise,   533
    He muste abstene from Rude & Unkunnyng,
And al suche vnthrifty folkys despise,

and draw to the Wise.

    To th[e] moost wytty & wisest drawyng,
    By whome he may be in wisedam lernyng.   537
    Right as a king is grettest in noblenesse,
    So is wisdam moost best to his hignesse.   539

Mundus[2] non est perpetuus; ergo, cum poteritis bene facere, non differatis nitentes ad habendam famam bonam; hec ypocras.

(78)

The world won't last. So do good at once.

The worlde is [not] in perpetuite,   540
    Therfore, for to do wele, make no delay;

---

[1] MS. maliciam.   [2] MS. Mumdus.

And if ye wolbe in felicite,
   Put you in peyne and deuour
      To be in blissed fame while that ye may.   544
        It is a comon sawe, he that doth wele,   He who does good, shall
        Shal haue it by goode lawe, Reason & skyle.   546 get good.

Non sis dissipator sicut ignorans q*uod* h*a*beat ; nec
sis p*a*rcus vt non fias seruus ; se*d* in omnibus habeas
moderanciam, quia in om*n*ib*us* vtilis est mensura ; hec
Pitogoras
             (79)

Be nat in yo*u*re expenses ouer large,   547 Don't be a spendthrift
   Ne to sca[r]ce by maner of nygonship.[1]   or niggard,
A goode mesure, kepe euer in yo*u*r charge,   but ever moderate.
   Worshipfully longyng to yo*u*r lordeship,
      Eschewyng al dishonou*r* & shenship,   551
        That yo*u*r blessed name may spryng & florissh.
        [. . . . . . . *line omitted.*]   553

Ne sis suspiciosus ; quia suspicio int*er* te & amicor*um*
que*m*cum*que*, amorem abscindit ; hec Logmon.
             (80)

Amonges many thinges, oon thing kepe,   554 Don't be too suspicious,
   Not to be ouer meche suspecious,
Ner compasse, ner wade th*er*in ouer depe,
   For that is a conceyte sedicious,
      Bryngyng many a man right vertuous   558 or you'll lose folk's love.
        To dep*a*rte from the grete affeccioñ
        That he was of by goode entencioñ.   560

Amicus cognoscit*ur* in necessitatib*us*, quia in gaudio
quilibet est amicus ; hec Diogenes.
             (81)

A Freende is knowen in necessite ;   561 Need proves Friends.
   In Ioy, men may haue frend*es* plenteuous.
A man whan he is in felicite,
   To please hym, al men be right studious.
      In adu*er*site, men be nat Ioyous   565 A Friend in need shows his worth.
        To be freendly, w*ith*oute he be rigĥt goode,
        Wele disposed, and of natural bloode.   567

---

[1] niggardliness.

Regna perduntur propter quatuor. Quia si a Rege

(1)   neclīgantur Radices / et solummodo ad Ramorum guber-
nacula intendatur, Regna perdiunt ; & vt fortuitis atten-

(2)   datur fiduciis que expedirent omissis operibus Regna
perduntur ; et vt ad populacionem terre minime inten-

(3)   datur, Regna perduntur ; & propter diuternitatem bello-

(4)   rum, Regna perduntur ; hec Plato.

(82)

By foure thinges, loste is a Region :   568

   Tattende to youthe, and not to men of Age,

And daily batel by Rebellion,

   And truste to fortune / with-owte werke sage,

   And not tentende (thaugh he be high in sage)   572

     To the landes goode populacion.

     Thise foure / bene a Roialmes is destruccion.   574

Tua beneficia bonis collata, Retribucionem expetunt,
et impensa vili ad plura petenda inducunt ; hec Plato.

(83)

Your benefetis geuen to goode men,   575

   Asken daily grete retribucion.

That goode that is to euel folk geuen,

   Asken gretter multiplicacioñ ;

   For thei take not in reputacioñ   579

     No-thynge as goode, vertuous men wol do ;

     Therfore goode men bithe (*sic*) appliable so.   581

Non oportet Regem in eum despicientem confidere,
nec in avido[1] multum, nec in eo pro quo (*sic*) meruit
pena[m] et commisit errorem, nec in illo quem dominio
priuauit et bonis, nec in eo qui suo regimine passus est
dampna, nec in eo qui amiciciam contraxit cum inimico ;
ymmo necesse est talibus nullam concedere potestatem ;
& si est possibile eorum carere suffragio in nullo eis
incumbit ; hec Asseron.

(84)

A kyng shulde neuer put his confidende   582

   In any creature hym despisinge,

Ner in a couetous man-is sentence,

---

[1] MS. opido, but the English versions have "in him that is
covetous ;" and the following phrase is not rendered.

Ner in a man errynge, peine deseruing,
Ner in hym that hathe be of goode pryuyng,[1]   586
  Ner in hym that is hurt for his trespasse,
Nor in hym that is in your enemyes grace.   588

Whom a King
shouldn't
trust.

Decet Regem studiosum siue solic*i*tum e*ss*e, Requirere
suu*m* Regnu*m* et suu*m* popu*lum*, sicut do*min*u*s* orti
suu*m* Ortum requirit. & co*n*uenit Regi q*uo*d sit p*ri*mus
ostendere leges pe*r*tinentes popu*l*o, in bonu*m* exemplum
populi; he*c* Pitagoras.

(85)

A kynge shude be right besy and studious   589
  To gouerne his Roiaulme & his people pure,
As a Gardyner is right laborous
  To kepe his gardeyne clene from wedys seure,
  Leuyng[2] wele in Rightfulnesse to endure.   593
    A kyng sholde be fyrst kepynge his lawe;
    Al other must doo the same for his awe.   595

A King
should
govern his
Realm well,

and keep his
Laws him-
self.

Decet regem non multum app*r*eciare seip*s*um, nec
gubernari suo consilio, nec vti frequenter venacione, nec
incedere semita qua*m* ignorat, nec angusta, nec nocte
obscura; et q*uo*d sit hillaris vultus, & aspiciens libenter
homines, & salutet eos et q*uo*d placite conuerset*ur*, quia
popu*lus* multu*m* attendit ista; he*c* Pitagoras.

(86)

A kynge sholde not sett hym selfe in myche price, 596
  Ner his counseil haue of hym gouernance,
Ne ofte use huntyng, kepiug wele his trice,[3]
  Ner take any newe way by ignorance,
  Ner greuyng, ne by myght for surance,   600
    But gladsom of chere, al folk salutyng;
    Thanne al men wol be his highnesse blessyng. 602

A King
should
not hunt too
much,

and should be
civil to his
folk.

Fac om*n*ia cum consilio; he*c* Salamon.[4]

(87)

By advis and goode counseile to gouerne   603
  Is goode, but not to be i*n* gouernance
Of his counseil, but of theim for to lerne,

He shouldn't
let his Coun-
cil rule him.

---

[1] depriving.   [2] Believing.   [3] Station in huntyng.
[4] Caxton's Salon.

A King
should con-
sult wise folk.
And texecute your selfe in al substance ;

Thus ye may guide your selfe in assurance.   607

　And asketh of wise people ofte ;

　And that shal kepe your high estate a lofte.   609

　　Caueas a comedendo & bibendo a manu multum ha-
bencium zelotipiam, et ab aliis vilibus, nisi ab illis de
quorum securus est credencia et sensu, et qui diligunt
eum & dominium suum ; hec Pitagoras.

(88)

Don't eat and
drink with
jealous or
poor men.
And be ye ware of your etynge & drynkyng,   610

　Principally of men of gelousye,

And of symple wreches pourely lyuyng ;

　But drede never theim þat can rectifie

　Theim selfe, & wittily theim Iustifie,—   614

　　For suche personnes bene of grete credence,—

　　Ner theim that ye loue with grete diligence.   616

　　Si cum volueris aliquem corrigere, non te geras velut
homo optans de alio habere vindictam, ymmo agas velut
volens curare seipsum ; hec Diogenes.

(89)

Punish to
cure, not to
revenge.
If ye wol do any correccion,   617

　Behaue you not as ye wolde do vengeance,

But as ye wolde cure hym from Corrupcioñ,

　And so ye shal deserue of god pleasance,

　And kepe your selfe in blissed assurance.   621

　　For ye be a leche of Iniquite,

　　Chast[en]yng wronge bi felicite.   623

　　Sciatis pro certo quod timor dei est maior sapiencia
& maior delectacio & est illud a quo fluit omne bonum
& aperit portas intellectus et sensus legis et non poteritis esse iusti nisi habueritis timorem dei. Vtamini
sapiencia & sequimini legem assuescatis mansuetudinem
et ornetis vos bonis documentis & cogitetis bene in
vestris rebus et excludentur anime vestre a seruitute
ignorancie et seruitute Iuuentutis ; hec Hermes.

(90)

The fear of
God is the
best wisdom.
Knowe for certeyne that the dre[de] of Iesu   624

　is the grettest wisedam & dilectacion,

Of whiche springeth al goodenes & vertue,
  Of wise vnderstandyng exultacioñ,
  And of goode guidynge dom*i*nacioñ.   628
    So who that wolbe wytty & eke wise,
    Drede god, and he shal haue it in best guise. 630

Fear God, and you'll grow wise.

Fac filios tuos a sua pr*a*uitate addiscere, priusqu*am* pr*e*cedant multum & trahant*ur* a malicia, & non peccabitis in eis ; h*ec* Hermes.

(91)

Suche childred (*sic*) as ye haue in gou*er*nance,   631
  Whether thei be yo*ur* owne or other men-is,
While thei be yonge, put theim in assurance
  Of lernyng & vertuous doinges,
    Leeste in age thei wol make eschewyngis,   635
    And ye therof haue the synne & the charge,
    When first ye were at libertee & large.   637

Train children while they're young,

or they'll go wrong when old.

Cum festa celebrabitis existe[n]s hyllares in domib*us* ves*t*ris cum familia, Recordem*i*ni paup*er*um, largientes elemosinas & ben*e*ficia, & confortemini angustuosos & tristes ; Redimatis captiuos, curetis infirmos, induatis nudos, cibetis famelicos, sicientes potetis. Recipiatis p*er*igrinos, satisfaciat*is* Creditorib*us*, tueamini. iniu*r*ia*m* pacientes, non addatis affliccionem afflictis, y*m*mo confortemini & mutetis eos placitis et ornatis op*er*ib*us* ; h*ec* Hermes.

(92)

Ay the werkys of m*er*cy haue in mynde,   638
  Especially the poure & the heuy,
And lete not god fynde you herin vnkynde,
  But in obseruance herof beth besy,
    Whiche ye [are] bounden to do sekerly.   642
      For on a day ye shul make rekenyng,
      How of thise dedys ye haue made guidyng.   644

Be merciful to the poor.

One day you shall give account of your deeds.

Cauete a societate malor*um* & inuidior*um*, ebrior*um* & ignorantu*m* ; h*ec* hermes. (C.)
  Malo te non associes, q*ui*a tua natura absq*ue* tui noticia aliq*u*id subripiet de natura ipsius ; hec Plato.

(93)

Don't asso-
ciate with
envious or
drunken folk.

Associe you nat with men enuious,   645
  Dronkelowe, ignorant, ne of Il nature,
But with the best, ay most vertuous,
  Of whom ye shal haue no shame ne lesure;
  Of Il, ye may haue of vertue rupture.   649
    Yf ye desire to come to famous name,
    Kepe this as ye luste to esche your blame.   651

Non iurare faciatis mendaces, quia participes eritis
peccatorum quando scietis eum veritatem denegasse.
Eciam decet Regem non vti homine men[daci] nec
prauo; hec Hermes.

(94)

Don't make a
liar swear.

Yf ye knowe a lesyngmonger and fals,   652
  Make hym not swere; he is of no credence;
Yf ye do, ye be in synne als;

Banish all
such.

Exile al suche owte of your high presence;
  Suche doon many tymes grete diligence   656
    To make discorde, debate & variance,
    When goode vnite sholde be & pleasance.   658

Si percipiatis in aliquo aliquam lesionem vel aliquam
maculam, non dehonestatis vel derideatis eum, sed rece-
datis ad deum quod omnes estis creati ex vna materia;
& qui deridet, non assecuratur, vt ad tempus non incidit
in idem, quia decet, quum videritis, eleuare oculos ad
deum, gratifica[n]tes eidem de salute vobis concessa, &
petentes misericordiam, quod vos custodiat & caue[at]
a derisione, quia per hoc nascitur odium; hec Hermes.

(95)

Don't laugh
at a disfig-
ured man.

Yf ye finde any spotte, fylth, or lesion[1]   659
  In any personne or in creature,
Dishonnour hym not with derision:
  Ye be nat in suche suerte ne mesure,
  But that the same may happ to you ful sure.   663
    Therfore, if ye stande in case resonable,
    Thanke god that ye nat therof culpable.   665

---

[1] injury.

Tria sunt op*era* sapientis, facere de inimico amic*um*,
de nesciente scientem, de malo bon*um* ; hec Hermes.

(96)

Thre thinges longen to a wytty man,	666 A wise man
That is, in wisdam & sapience,	
To make of an enemye, a frende that cañ	turns foes into friends,
be lovyng w*ith* a frendeli diligence ;	
And of vnkonnyng, to be in grete science ;	670 fools into wise men,
And of il disposed in wykkednesse,	and ill-disposed folk
To be reconsiled to blissednesse.	672 into good ones.

Nullus debet d*omi*nari, nisi pius. Decet reges non
dare posse, nec d*omi*nium, nisi pietatem habentibus ; et
ex hoc diliget omnes, sicut bonus pater, bonos filios ;
hec Hermes.

(97)

A king aught not to geue auctorite,	673 Give authority only to merciful and just men.
Might, power, lordeship, ne also puissance,	
But to piteous men of Equite,	
For no praier, grete requeste or instance.	
Rigorous men make grete disseuerans.	677
Ye shul loue al forlkes (*sic*) in charite,	
As the fader the sone w*ith* grete pite.	679

Vita hominis est tam breuis q*uo*d quis non ha*b*eret[1]
aliu*m* in odio ; hec hermes. Et tractetis amicos[2] v*est*ros
cu*m* amore vero, nec ostendatis vna hora signum odii.
Socrates.

(98)

Considre that yo*ur* liff is shorte and brief	680 As your life is short
In this transitory world and passing ;	
Therfore, for a goode & blessed relieff,	
Ye aught not to haue other in hatyng,	don't hate any one, but cherish all.
But hertely cherissh theim w*ith*oute prating,	684
Neither wronging theim bi extorcioñ,	
Ner plukking theim als bi compulsion.	686

Qui non bene faciat Amicis cu*m* potest, deser*en*t eum
cum indigebit eisdem ; hec Plato.

-----

[1] MS. haberent.   [2] MS. tragemicos.

(99)

Cherish your
friends, and
show your
love to em
daily.

Cherissh wele yo*u*r freendes while that ye may,   687

    As wele in worde as p*r*eferrying,

Showying theim semblance of love eue*r*y day,

    Corogeng theim to be to you lovyng.

Thus yo*u*r glorious fame shal be springing   691

    To high & lowe, of yo*u*r noble kyndnesse.

Who is he that wold nat please yo*u*r highnesse ?

Tria sunt que Regib*us* obsunt, supe*r*flua vini potacio,
Musicor*um* frequens auditu*s*, & amor nimis mulie*r*u*m* ;
hec hermes.

(100)

Kings must
not drink too
much, hear
music too
often, or care
greatly for
women.

Thre thinges bene contrary to a kyng,   694

    To be in supe*r*flue drinkyng of wyne,

And of musyke to haue to ofte hering,

    And to be to women in love-is pyne,[1]

Whiche hath brought many a man to Ruyne.   698

    Al suche thing noyant to yo*u*r high estate,

Eschewe al wey, if ye be fortunate.   700

Rex qui suu*m* regnu*m* statuit seruu*m* legis, debet
regnare ; et qui legem subiectam Regno efficit, Regnum
angustiat*ur* propter eum ; hec Ar*is*totel*e*s.

(101)

The King
that enforces
just laws,
shall reign
in peace.

That kyng that maketh his Region̄   701

    To be obedient to his iuste lawe,

That[2] reigne peasibly in an vnyon̄.

He that makethe his lawe souget to awe

Or to his Roialme, his wyt is not worth a strawe.

    He that dwelle in grete p*r*osperite,

Must obey lawe, and therto subget be.   707

Quando volueris consulere aliqu*em* sup*er* fac*t*is tuis,
Inuestiga illum qualiter seips*um* gubernet in suis ; q*ui*a
si videris eum non dirigere an*im*am suam, nec studere,
q*uo*d aliquas bonitates adquirat, multo plus tui negligens
erit, cu*m* te minori precio reputet qu*a*m seip*su*m ; hec
Socrates.

[1] anguish

[2] ? does.   *The* to do.   See *vn-the* 78/784.   Or is *That* for *Shal* ?

(102)

If ye wol aske counsaile of any mañ,　　　　　708

  Serche fyrste of his owne p*roper* gouerna[n]ce.

If he be not wele disposed, ner can

  Putte hymselfe in goode assurance,

    How shuld [ye] put in suche oon affiance?　712

      That[1] can nat be to hym selfe p*ro*ffitable,

      He shal not be to other availeable.　　　714

Don't consult any man till you find what he is in private.

Sis vigilans in tuo consilio, quia dormire in eo est
p*ar*ticipare cu*m* morte ; hec Pitagoras.

(103)

In yo*ur* counsail be quick and ay wakyng.　　715

  Who shold tendre so meche yo*ur* owne availle

As yo*ur* self? or els more Reasons making

  To yo*ur* entencion that myght p*re*vaille,

  And therto w*ith* al diligence travaile,　　　719

    That best knoweth yo*ur* estate & pleasance,

    And how it may best be had in assurance,　721

Be watchful and quick in counsel.

Caueas ne innitaris tui *tan*tu*m* co*n*silio, s*ed* consulas
qui fu*er*it bone discreci*on*is & ctatis prouecte, qui in
pluribus est expertus ; & pluriu*m* vtaris consilio & in-
uento, quod rectu*m* sit in aliquo eoru*m*, illud assumas,
alioquin vtilioribu*s* consilio comp*re*hensis ab om*ni*
h*a*bito p*er* te dirigas, et deus te diriget ; hec Hermes.

(104)

Trust neu*er* to yo*ur* owne wytte, ne in Counseil,　722

  But of aged men in discrecioñ,

Being experte of thrifty antiquaile ;

  And by meche aduis and inquisicioñ

  Of the moost wisest, take[2] discrecioñ,　　　726

    That nought eschape bi Innocencye,

    Neither bi negligence, ne by foly.　　　　728

Trust only aged men for counsel.

Quare sensatus petit consilium? Quia sui volun[ta]-
tem veretur, que suo sensui sine racioni miscet*ur* ; hec
Socrates.

(105)

Why dothe a wytty man aske counsaile?　　　729

  For he is ashamed of his owne wille,

A sensible man seeks counsel,

---

[1] That = who, he that.　　　　[2] MS. tate.

lest his own
wits fail him.

Leest his owne wytt & Reasoñ do hym faile,
 And brynge hym to grete shame and for to spille,
  Sith his owne Reason wil his owne wille fille. 733
  A wise Man wol nat put great affiance
  In his oune discretion ne constance. 735

Non est danda potestas super se,[2] quia si dederis
potestatem amico, vt suos pedes tuis pedibus superponat,
superponet in crastinum collo tuo ; hec Diogenes.[1]

(106)

Don't set any
one over you,

Yeue neuer power ne auctorite 736
 To no maner personne on erthe lyvyng
Vppon your self for any freilte.
 If ye be to any man licencyng
 To set his fote vpon youres areryng, 740

or he'll put
his foot on
your neck.

  He wol after set his fote vppon your nekke.
  [. . . . . . . *line omitted.*]

Oportet dominum secedere a populo suo, & non fami-
liariter conuersari cum eis. Alioquin despicietur, cum de
natura populorum sit despicere se inuicem, & conuer-
santes cum eis, unde *quemlibet conuersantem vnum et
idem Reputant sibi Ipsius.*[2] Nimia familiaritas[3] parit
contemptum ; hec Plato.

(107)

A Lord
mustn't be
too familiar
with folk.

A lorde shold nat be over conuersant 743
 With folke, ne in familiarite,
Leest they be to his honnour repugnant,
 And haue hym in despite of freilte,
 After nature of theire Iniquite. 747
  For to meche humblesse, vsed of olde,
  Makethe meche people to be over bolde. 749

Non intromittas te nisi de veris rebus, vt sint tua
opera veritas & non derisio ; hec Hermes. Et assume
illos in amicos qui veritatem sectantur ; hec Pitagoras.

(108)

Take part
only in true
things.

Entremete you neuer of other thing 750
 But of trewe withowte any soubtelte.

---

[1] Caxton gives this quotation as applying to wives particularly.
[2] Underlined in MS. [3] MS. familialitas.

And that your werkes be of trewe meanyng,
  Withoute derision or nycete,
    Whiche shal put you in grete tranquillite. 754
      For god is trouthe, & louyth it moost best,   God is Truth.
      And of all vertues is most surest. 756

Sapiencia adquiritur humilitas, bona voluntas, pietas
& priuacio peccatorum. Non recte agit qui querit Sapienciam non legendo; et ille qui cogitat habere eam
cum multa habilitate, est ignorans; hec Hermes.

(109)

By wisdam is goten humilite;   757   Wisdom
  And of many synnes priuacioñ,   begets
Meche other grete vertues & pite.   Humility,
  Wisdam must haue grete applicacioñ
  In meche redyng and other laboracioñ. 761
    It wol not be gotyn bi Ignorance,   and is got
                                 only by
    But with diligence & goo[d] gouuernance. 763   Diligence.

Bonum consilium ostendit In principio finem rei;
hec Socrates.

(110)

Goode & trewe counseille is of this nature :   764   Good counsel
  In euery mater atte begynnyng,   sees at fiıst
The eende is knowen perfitely & sure,   how a matter
  Wheder it wol perissh or be duryng,   will end.
    The verray sothe in al thinge concludyng. 768
      Therfore goode Counseil is necessary,
      That wol guide hym wele, & not miscary. 770

Qui obseruat Secretum est discretus & qui patefacit
est insipiens. Oportet hominem occultare Secretum
quod si reuelatur (*sic*) & magis gratus est ille, qui occultat licet ex secreto non obligetur, et occultare secretum
est nobilitas anime. *Cum tuum secretum cor tuum non*
continet multum minus tenebitur in cordibus aliorum ;[1]
hec Socrates.

(111)

To be secrete is a noble vertue;   771   Secresy is a
  And he that is a blabber is nat wise.   noble virtue.

[1] Underlined in MS.

Secretnesse pleasith almyghti Ihesu ;
   Where the contrari men greatly despise,
   A secrete man is discrete in that guyse.   775

If you don't keep your own secrets, who else will?
     He that can not kepe his owne secretnesse,
     How shold a nother kepe it in sadnesse ?   777

Cotidie addiscit homo experiendo que contingunt ;
sufficit homini scire que intuetur de contingentibus
mundo, & per id die quolibet potest nouam scienciam
habere ; hec Socrates.

(112)

Al day men may lerne by experience   778
   To se of euery werke the conclusioñ.

Honour follows good guidance,
Of goode guydyng & blessed diligence
   Sewith worship and goode direccioñ.

despising bad.
Of vnthriftynesse is despeccioñ.   782
    Therfore euery man may wele knowe & se,
    As he dothe, so shal he thriue or vnthe.   784

Deum recto amore diligens & amans sapienciam ipsius
et opera bona. Deus honorat eum, & curiosus est bene-
facit eidem ; hec Aristoteles.

(113)

God honours those who love Him.
Suche men as louen god with Rightful love,   785
   And his wisdam and goode werkes also,
God wol honnour theim, & set them aboue,
   And is curious, doyng wele theim to,
   Endowyng theime with plentuous grace so,   789
    That god wolbe euer thair protectour,
    In al tymes of nede and dependour.   791

Alium rectificare si poteris cupiat sicut cupis rectificare te ipsum, quia honor est & nobilitas anime tue.
Aristoteles. (C). Oportet dominum rectificare prius seipsum quam populum suum ; hec Zelon.

(114)

Set others right, as you would be set right.
Rectifie a noþer, if that ye may,   792
   As ye wolde your selfe be rectified.
And rectifie youre selfe first euery day,

Thus blessedly to be Iustified,   Do right,

By whiche grete noblesse is multiplied,   796

   Bothe in honnour, rightfulnesse & grete fame,

   Purchasyng you[1] therby a blessed name.   798   and win a blessing.

Si amorem tuum volueris cum aliquo durabile esse,
eum bene agendo informes ; hec Enesius.

(115)

Yf ye wol that your loue be with man durable,   799   To make folk love you, do good to them.

   Enfourme hym to do wele with grete stering,

For vertue shal euer be pardurable,

   Where vice shalbe abhorred & hatyng,

   And euer be in trouble & crakyng.[2]   803

     Loue standith in god & in his swetnesse,

     And wol not be had but in blessidnesse.   805

(116)

Amonges your other soubgettes al,   806   Prefer your own servants before outsiders.

   Your owne seruantes preferre & avaunce,

Bothe spiritual and eke temporal,

   Suche of your owne bringyng vppe in substance,

   In whom ye may stande in trewe assurance   810

     Of body and goode their l[i]ffes duryng,

     Redy at al tymes to youre pleasyng.   812

Potens est homo suos dirigere cum agnouerit seipsum,[3]
nam excellentis est sapiencie hominem sui ipsius habere
noticiam, nec ex dileccione quam habet in seipso fal-
latur et bonum se reputet cum non sit ; videmus enim
plures reputare se robustos et liberales, cum non sint, et
vniuersaliter, quasi omnes discreciores aliis reputant.
Et qui in se cogitat ista, minoris discrecionis existat ;
hec Galienus.

(117)

To knowe hymself is a vertuous thing,   813   Know your self,

   First to godward & to the world also ;

Than he is myghty hym self directyng,   and then you can rule others.

   Bryngyng al other goode gouernance to,

   With many noble direccions, so   817

---

[1] MS. your.   [2] crying out.   [3] Underlined in MS.

Want of self-
knowledge
brings an ill
name.

That it shal be to his glorious fame,
Where not to knowe hymself may haue Il name.

Q*uis* est i*ustu*s et q*uis sensatus ?* Justus est ille q*ui
potest iniusticia*m *ajere, & non agit;* & sensatus sive
discret*us* est Rex om*n*i[s] *qui nouit id qu*o*d humana
natura sufficit;* hec Galienus.

(118)

He is just,
who can do
wrong, but
does right.
He is dis-
creet, who
knows men's
nature.

Who is iuste, who is discrete & wytty ?   820
   He is iuste, that may do wronge, & dothe right.
He is discrete, that know*eth* p*e*rfitly
   Al thing after Manne-is nature & myght.
   Therfore alwey, in eu*ery* man-is sight,   824
     Attempre you to be iuste & discrete,
     Whiche bene to yo*ur* high mageste mete. 826

Vt non irascatur homo, memoretur assidue qualit*er*
sua non interest vt obedia*tur* ei continue, sed vt qu*isque*
obediat, nec vt serui*atur* ei iugit*er*, se*d* vt aliqu*i* alteri
seruiat, nec vt inferat*ur* eidem; et q*uo*d deus circum-
spicit om*n*ia qui*bus* co*n*sideratis non vexaberis ira, vel
modico turbeberis si turberis; h*ec* Tesilius.

(119)

You are not
alway to be
obeyd,

Ayainste wrathe & Ire is a remedy   827
   To remember, that it is nat leful
Not to contynue in obstinance
   To be obeyed, but to-beie[1] rightful;   [1 to obeie]
   Ner to be serued, but serue skylful   831

but must
obey God and
man in due
season.

     Thinges, & to be in obedience
     To god and man in their deue existence. 833

(120)

If a man
offends in
one thing,
don't hold
him all bad.

Yf a man haue offended in oon thing, 834
   Repute hym not in al thinge culpable.
There is no man so wele hym behauyng,
   But he may be in some thyng chargeable;
   Yet the case may be Remediable. 838

Take every
man at his
best.

     So co*n*sidre eu*ery* man for the best:
     Thus ye shul lyve cheritably in rest. 840

Cu*m* inimico pacificare studeas, licet fortitudinis et
tue potencie sis securus; h*ec* Maedarges.[1]

(121)

To pacificie yo*ur* enemye, be studious, 841

 Thaugh of youre strengh & power ye be seure,

Whiche is a dilige*n*ce right gracious,

 Causyng you in tranquillite tendure

In confourmyng you to holy scripture. 845

 Syche as a man sekythe, so shal he haue;

 If he seke peas and Rest, god wol hym saue. 847

Strive to make peace with your foe.

If you seek Peace, God will save you.

Si rex egerit iustum & Rectum pop*u*li sui, principa-
bit*ur* animis; et si iniustu*m* & iniquu*m* co*m*miserit
ip*s*um suu*m* Regem ostendit exte*r*ius, se*d* ad aliu*m*
p*r*incipantem ip*s*or*um* corda dec[l]inant (*sic*); hec
Enesius.

(122)

Yf a kyng do iustly & Righ[t]fully, 848

 He standithe wele in the peoples conceyte.

Yf he do wyckedly & wrongfully,

 He p*ur*chasethe hym in grete deceyte,

And for kynge they wolde haue hym in Receite, 852

 Howe be it that they haue hym not in love,

 Willyng that he shold never he a-bove? 854

A King who does right is lovd; one

who does wrong is tolerated but not lovd.

Qui te bonu*m* existimat, eu*m* stude Reputare veri-
dicu*m*; & pro bono[2] ha*b*eas qui te p*ro* bono elegit, siue
sit humilis siue altus. Non potest multis p[re]cip*ere*,
qui anime sue no*n* p*r*ecepit cu*m* sit vna; hec Enesius.

(123)

Yf any people holde you v*er*tuous, 855

 Goode, gentil, kinde, curteise wit*h* al mekenesse,

To repute hym trewe be right labourous,

 Whether he be lowe or in grete highnesse.

He that hathe grete labo*ur* & besynesse, 859

 How shold he reule and gou*er*ne many moo?

 [. . . . . *line omitted.*] 861

If you're thought good, strive to be good.

In mu*n*do n*i*hil dete*r*ius est q*uam* gene*r*ositate &
doctrina carere; h*ec* Maedarg*es*.

---

[1] Caxton's Sacdarge.   [2] MS. bone.

ASHBY.   M

(124)

The worst thing is lack of learning and gentleness.

The worst thing of al this wide World is[1] this, [1 MS. in]
To lakke doctrine and also gentilnesse.   863
Uncunning show*eth* grete lewednesse, y-wis
Gentilnesse considereth al goodenesse,
Who that lakkithe it muste falle in distresse.   866
These vertues haueth wele in yo*ur* mynde,
That the p*r*ofittes of theim ye may fynde.   868

Oportet que*m*libet assudue scrutari ope*r*a sua, & scire niti qu*od* refrena*ntur* de eo vicini, et hii sp*ecialiter* qui me*r*cantur et conu*er*santur cu*m* eo, & in quo vitup*er*ant aut laudant eundem; quia cu*m* incedit tali via, non latebit eu*m* aliquid vicio*rum* suo*rum*; hec Aristotiles.

(125)

Find out what folk say of you,

Men shuld serche often the opynyon   869
That men wol saien of there goue*r*nance,
Eyther preising or makyng obieccioñ,
Wherof thei shuld be in ful assurance
Of what reule þei be in substance,   873

and amend what is wrong.

Where-vpon thei may guide theime in suche wise
To amende theime, and to be holden wise.   875

Serve God in 10 ways.
1. 2.
3. 4.
5. 6.
7. 8. 9.
10.

Decem modis de[o] se*r*uit*ur*, & su*nt* hii: Grati*a*s age si aliqu*id* impendit*ur* t*ibi*; Si male ha*b*ueris, s[us]tine pacienter; Si loqueris, loqu*are* ve*r*itate*m*; Quod promi-seris, p*er*fice. Si iudicau*er*is, Recte iudica; mensuram ha*b*eas siq*uam* potes; Benefacias priusq*uam* requiraris; Amicum honora, Indulgeas amici & inimici errori. Non nisi quod t*ibi* vis, amico consideres; hec Arcules (*sic*).

(126)

In ten Mane*r* wise god must be se*r*ued,   876
Euel thing*es* suffre paciently,
For to speke truly must be ose*r*ued.

1. Suffer patiently.
2. Speak truth.
3. Perform promises.
4. Judge justly.
5. Be moderate.
6. Give before you're askt.

Yche p*r*omisse must be p*er*formed truly;
Iche iugement must be deuided iustly.   880
Kepe eue*r*more conable mesure;
Er ye required, doo goodenesse sure.   882

(127)

Showe to al maner freindis grete honnour,   883

  Thankyng god of his yefte & benignite ;

And pardon freendes & vnfreendes errour ;

  And desire neuer of your frende to be

Other than ye wolde the same in you see.   887

   And thise ten thinges kepe euer suerly.

Thus keping your self to god demeurly.   889

7. Honour your friends. 8. Thank God. 9. Forgive friend and foe. 10. Expect no more than you'd give.

Cum tua discrecio prohibuerit aliquid te facturum, inobediens esse non debes ; quia maius peccatum quod potest accidere est quod investiget te id agere quod vetauit ; hec Plato.

(128)

When your discrecioñ forbedith thing   890

  For to be doon in eny maner wise,

Therto ye shuld not be disobeying ;

  For it is gretter synne, I promisse,

  To do ayeinste conscience in suche guise,   894

   Whiche shal frete and gruge in your soule & mynde,

  And daily to grete repentance you bynde.   896

When you forbid anything, don't do it yourself.

Ex tribus cognoscitur sapiens,[1] quod per ea que nouit ; quod non se magno habeat precio, nec ob vituperantem aliquem irascatur, nec cum laudatur fiat elatus ; hec Plato.

(129)

By thre thinges is knowen a wiseman,   897

  That he repute not hym selfe in grete price,

And that from wrathe he him self restreine can

  Whan he is set at nought & holden nyce ;

  And whan he is preised in noble wise,   901

   Not to be elate ne in pride therfore,

  But in grete pacience & mekenesse more.   903

A wise man is known by—1. not thinking too much of himself; 2. not getting angry at dispraise; 3. not being puft up by praise.

Cum rex vincit suos inimicos, oportet eum sequi bonas consuetudines, scilicet in iusticia, in largitate pecunie, in paciencia, in diligencia, et in aliis consu[e]- tudinibus bonis ; hec hermes.

[1] MS. sapience.

(130)

If a King
conquers his
foes, he must
be liberal,

Yf god sende you in this world victory   904
    Of your enemyes by your manhode,
Ye muste kepe in your noble memory
    Goode noble custumes vsed of olde :
    In largenesse of money be right bolde ;   908

patient, just,
and diligent.

    In pacience, iustice and diligence,
    Do your peyne to haue true experience.   910

Cum seruieris alicui domino, noli fieri equalis sibi, nisi in fide, in sensu, in paciencia, in aliis vero nequaquam caueas, ne te aspiciat sibi equalem in statu, aut vestitu, aut in suis deliciis ; hec Plato.

(131)

Let a servant
equal his lord
in Faith, Wit,
and Patience,

A seruaunt shold nat be euen equal   911
    To his lorde, but in thre thinges trewly, .
That is, in feithe, wytte, & pacience al,

not in State,
Dress, or
Luxuries.

    Not in estate nor clothinges richely,
    Ner in other delites excessely ;   915
    But iche man knowe hym self and his degre,
    Non excedyng for possibilite.   917

Si quesieris facere facere (*sic*) despeccionem inimico ; non offendas teipsum pro inimico ; hec pitagoras.

(132)

If you despise
your foe,

Yf ye propose to make despeccioñ   918
    To youre enemy bi any greuance,

take care you
don't hurt
yourself by it.

Beware ye make no suche offencioñ
    To hurte your self for suche wilful vengeance ;
    But kepithe in your noble remembrance,   922
    To attemper you in suche maner wise
    That no hurte of your enemy arise.   924

Bonus gratificat de bonis receptis iuxta possibili[t]atem conferentis et satisfaccionem recipientis. vilis vero non gratificat nisi iuxta qualitatem benefactorum ; hec Plato.

(133)

A good man
thanks every
giver accord-
ing to his
ability.

A goode man thanketh euery benefete,   925
    After the yeuers possibilite.
Vile & euel men be other-wise sett,

For to thanke aftur the quantite

Of benefit, what euer it be ; 929

So goode men haue gentil condicion,

And Il men other dispocis*ion*. 931

A bad man looks only to the quantity of the gift.

Aliqui Reges ha*b*ent p*r*o bono conseruare semp*er* statum vn[i]us gen*er*is ex subditis tantu*m*, et in hoc valde falluntur et errant, q*uia* vnu*m* genus ho*m*inu*m* non nec*cessar*io est in condicione & statu eodem, y*m*mo minuunt*ur*, bonitas ip*s*ius assimilans terre in qua serit*ur* continue semen vnius gen*er*is, q*uo*d temporis p*r*ocessu corru*m*pit*ur* et imitatur ; hec Plato.

(134)

Sum kynges conseruen[1] alwey ooñ kynde 932

Of yo*ur* (*sic*) soubgett*is*, & theime meche p*r*eferre

Oonly, and noon other haue in theire mynde,

Wherin thei be deceyued and meche erre,

For men of other kynde may be more derre. 936

Man-is kinde is right meche chaungeable,[2]

As sede often sowen is mutable. 938

Some kings favour but one kind of their subjects,

tho' others may be better.

Bonu*m* est loqui dic*er*e modicu*m* Rac*ion*e, completum est respondere laudabilit*er* et confestim ; hec A*r*i*stote*les.

(135)

Grete wisdam is, litil to speke, 939

Pronuncing wele & complete of reason,

Anoon with laudable aunswere & make,

Hauing regar*d*e to iche tyme & season ;

To meche language hauith in geason[3] 943

Alweyes spekyng w*ith* aduisement,

Bestowyng yo*ur* vttrance to goode entent. 945

To talk little is wisdom.

Fornicator laudari non potest, nec e*ss*e *h*illar*i*s ira-cundus, nec *liberalis inuidus, nec cupidus esse diues ;* [4] hec A*r*i*stote*les.

(136)

A fornicato*ur* may not be preised, 946

Ner a Ireful man to be meche gladful,

Ner a liberal man to be seised

Don't praise a fornicator.

---

[1] MS. corseruen. [2] MS. claungeable.

[3] The adj. meaning "scarce" used as a substantive.

[4] Underlined in MS.

In envye, nor the couetouse richeful.

Thise thinges be thus ordeyned righful ;   950

Man is purified by his works.

For, as golde is pured by fire craftly,

So is man bi his workes feithfully.   952

Sapiencia exornat diuitis diuicias, et pauper*is* paupertatem occultat ; hec A*r*istote*l*es.

(137)

Wisdom adorns riches, hides poverty,

Wisdom exorneth nobli the richesse   953

Of a Richeman, and hideth pouer*te*

Of a pore man, being in wrechednesse.

What may be more felicite

Then to be wytty in prosper*i*te ?   957

and excels all else.

When ye haue serched al the worlde aboute,

Wisdam excellithe other wi*th*owte doubte.   959

Hominis lingua sue discrecionis est Scriba ; q*uia* q*ui*dq*ui*d dici volu*er*it, ip*s*a sc*r*ibit ; & co*m*pescere lingu*a*m est v*ir*tus p*r*ima ; hec Ar*i*stote*l*es.

(138)

Restraint in speech is the first virtue.

The first v*er*tue is to kepe man-is tong,   960

For it is scribe of his discrecio*n* ;

For what it wol say, it writith at longe.

By sure tonge, al noble direccio*n*

Ys assured, and al[1] correccio*n*,   [1 MS. al &]   964

Thaugh it be bi the swerde or bi iustice.

The wise tong co*m*manndeth þ*a*t shal suffice. 966

Non est apud Regem minus decenci*us* quam predari, cu*m* Regis intersit vice patris se gerere ; hec Ar*i*stote*l*es.

(139)

Plundering by a King is disgraceful.

On erthe ther is no thing so vnsemyng   967

As a kynge to be in predacio*n*,

Or by co*m*pulsion to be taking,

Sith in hym shold be al saluacio*n*,

And as a fader in probacio*n* ;   971

Who shold be the people-is protecto*u*r,

But oonly the kyng & their defendo*u*r.   973

Mali timore obediu*n*t, boni beneficio ; ergo hos duos modos agnoscens, libent*er* vni beneficia ; Reliq*u*o ve*r*o penam infligas ; hec Ar*i*stote*l*es.

(140)

Euel men, for drede done obedience ;   974

    Good men doon soo for benefete truly.

Of thise too thinges hauing experience,

    Doo to the toon, benefettes freely,

And to the tother, punysshment iustly.   978

    Thus, bi your witty disseuerance,

    Ye shul make men tobey their legeance.   980

Bad men obey for fear; good, to do good.

Benefaciendo populo domineris, quia tuum dominium durabilius erit, prouide quam aggrauando eosdem ; nam cum eorum dominareris ante corporibus, deinde domina-beris animis propter beneficia que concedis. & scias quod populus dicto presumptuosus, facile ad factam collabitur ; igitur nitere quod non labatur ad dictam, & sequitur quod non ad factam labetur ; hec Aristoteles.

(141)

In dowynge wele to the people ofte tyme,   981

    Your maieste shal be more durable

Than in grevyng theime, theire dedis to lyme.[1]

    For where their bodies were appliable

To youre highnesse in al thinge prophetable,   985

    Now thei shul be in body & soule

    For your benefite in feire & fowle.   987

Be kind to your folk, and you'll reign long.

(142)

For certaine, the people presumptuos   988

    In wordis, wol slyde to dedys lightly ;

Therfore be ye therin right laberous,

    That folk slyde nat to wordes wykedly,

In eschewyng theire dedes iniustly :   992

    A king aught to haue a wise prouision

    To kepe his folk in goode direccion.   994

People presumptuous in word, will soon be so in deed.

Obseruatores fidei siue leges Fideles promoueas, et ex hoc Reputaberis in hoc mundo compositus, et in alio finem eonsequeris optatum ; & malos refrena, quia, cum hoc, et leges diriges & populum ; hec Aristoteles.

[1] limit

(143)

Promote
keepers of
faith and
law,

Cherisshe kepers of the feithe & iuste Lawe,   995
  Referryng theim to grete promocioñ,
And refreine Ivel men with fere & awe ;
  And thus ye make goode direccioñ
Of the lawe, & kepe folk in subieccioñ,   999

and you'll
have your
realm in
peace.

  An[d] eke kepe your Roialme in tranquillite,
  Restful peas, comfort & feelicite.   1001

Quam turpe est pronunciare aliquod, et opere non
complere ; & quam pulcrum apparere operibus prius
dictis ; hec Tholomeus.

(144)

How bad it is
to speak good
and not do it!

How fowle, how vnhappy it is, to speke   1002
  Perfitly, & not be in dede ;
And how feire, and how goode and polletike,
  Firste the people to goode werkes theim lede,
And therafter to speke, is right grete mede.   1006
    Whan euery goode man-is dede is before,
    Than euery goode speche accordeth therfore. 1008

Philosophi dixerunt Alexandro imperatori, quomodo
in etate tam tenera[1] potuisti, & vt regna perquirere.
Respondit : quia reconsilians inimicos amicos feci, &
amicis beneficiis satisfeci ; hec Tholomeus.

(145)

Alexander
said

Philosophers asked a questioñ   1009
  Of kyng Alex[an]dre, the Emperour,
How in his tendre age in possession

he got his
Realms
by reconcil-
ing his foes,
and doing
good to his
friends.

  Hathe goten mony Realmes with fauour.
He onswered, by two meanes with honnour,   1013
    Oon to reconsile his enemyes,
    Another to do wele to his freindes.   1015

Si regis consultor & phisicus eiusdem in cunctis vota
sequantur, dampnificabitur semper, et erit infirmus con-
tinuo boni finis exspec[ta]cione fraudatus ; hec Asseron.

(146)

If a King's
adviser and
doctor follow
his will,

Yf a Counselor or phisicioñ   1016
  Of a kynge folowe his wille & entente,

---

[1] MS. teneri.

At al tymes of his direccioñ,

The king is nat suer of goode Aduisement,

Ner of his body helthful amendement.   1020

    Therfor thise two *per*sonnes haue grete charge

    To be trewe & playne to thair king at large. 1022

he'll get neither good advice nor a healthy body.

Decet Regem sua negocia illi *com*mittere q*ue*m fidem
et sensu p*ro*bauit; et si talem habere non poterit, q*ui*
cu*m* sapientib*us* & bonis[1] conue*r*satus est, illi com-
mittat; hec Asseron.

(147)

A king sholde wisely his nedes *com*mitte   1023

    To hym that he had often approved

In grete witte and wisedam, & hym not remitte

    Vnto no folkes to be reproved.

    Yf he cannot to suche folk be confourmed,   1027

      Than, to suche folk as be conversant

      W*ith* goode men and wise, to Il repugnant. 1029

Kings should employ only wise folk,

or those knowing them.

Qui sp[l]endide viuit *cum* Rege et *per*sistit magni-
fice, Impossibile est in aliq*ue*m no*n* conuenire defectu*m*,
p*ro*pt*er* quod, Regem Sapientem esse oportet vt *cum*
aliqu*em* audierit de suis contra se *com*misisse delictum.
Hora non transeat quin de veritate aut falsitate constet
eidem. Et *s*imiliter de quant[it]ate delicti, & si conscie*n*-
cia fue*r*it aut errore commissum, et si condicionis est talis
q*uo*d ad illud redeat, vel non indulgendo; hec Asseron·

(148)

Who that is wele cherisshed w*ith* a king,   1030

    And is w*ith* hym grete & splendiferous,

And hathe al thinge at his *com*maunding,

    It is impossible to be laborous

    To finde any grete defaulte odious.   1034

      Therf[or]e a kinge must make prouisioñ

      To haue lowe men to that entencioñ.   1036

Kings' grandest nobles won't

find out hateful defects;

but lower men can.

(149)

A wise king aught to haue trewe knowleging   1037

    Of al thinge a-yenste hym conspired,

Kings ought to know of all conspiracies against them.

[1] MS. bonus.

Withoute delaye, not oon houre over passinge,

    And that no tyme be loste ne ex_l_ired,

        Of the trouthe as it shold be required,   1041

        Aftur the quantite and condicion,

        Either for peine or remision.   1043

Regi famulantib*us* expedit suam ostendere virtutem
et fidem et nobilitatem generis, vt conscius Rex status
et condicionis vn[i]us cuiusq*ue* ip*s*or*um*, cum eis poterit
sua promouere negocia, & vt expedit execucioni mandari.
Et si Rex obedienti & fideli, & e contra de merentib*us*
pro meritis no*n* respondet, vt aliqui ob retribucionem
vtant*ur*, & alii te*r*reant*ur* acerbitate penar*um*, nec Rex
reputari debet, nec agendor*um* director; h*ec* Asseron.

(150)

But a kynge rewarde eu*er*y man-is trouthe,   1044

    And in lyke wise punysshe a trespassoure,

His direccion ellis were grete Routhe.

    To take goode & Il in lyke fauour,

    Accordithe not wele to a Gouernour.   1048

        So take eu*er*y man aftur his des*er*te,

        Either in cherisshinge or in smert.   1050

Qui Regem a fraude non[1] eripit, & medico ueritatem
occultat, et debitum pandere secretum non pandit amico,
interimit seip*s*um ; hec Asseron.

(151)

Who that in Il chalengeth not a King,   1051

    And hidithe to his leche the verite,

And hidethe secretnesse from frende louyng,

    He must slee hymselfe, or ellis vnthe.

    To be playne & trewe is grete libertee ;   1055

        For trouthe at longe shal nev*er* be shamed,

        Thaugh he be other while Iuyl gramed.   1057

Si Rex felix constit*er*it, sua bene agent*ur* negocia ;
et si sapiens, sapiencia suo in tempore roborat*ur*; & si
verus, letabit*ur* p*o*p*ulus* ; & si iust*us*, sua regnac*i*o durat ;
h*ec* Asseron.

[1] MS. nor.

(152)

Yf a kyng be[1] blissed, al his nedes   [¹ MS. be be]   1058   The benefits
    Bene done wele to his proffit & honnour ;   of a King's
                                                  being blessed,
Yf he be wise, al thinges spedes ;   wise, true,
    Yf he be trewe, he is in man-is fauour ;   and just.
    Yf he be iuste, of right a supportour,   1062
      His Royalme & Region is durable,
      And his direccion commendable.   1064

Plurimum est graue Regnum adquirere, sed est scire
grauius conservare ; hec Asseron.

(153)

A king, any Region to conquere,   1065   It's hard to
    Is right costlowe, harde, peinful & greuous ;   conquer a
                                                 land ; but
But to conserue a Roylme is me more fere,   harder to
    And more wisdame & wytt, & more laborous,   keep it.
    Gretter prouision, and more tedious.   1069
      Better were a thing never to [be] had,
      Than in handes to quaile & to be badde.   1071

Expedit sapienti qui Regi adheret, vt si viderit eum
aliquid agere sibi aut Regno aut populo suo nociuum,
recitare historias & exempla que simili negocio contingunt, vt a tali facto desistat, Eo tamen referat modo
quod ille percipiat enunciata pro eo ; hec Asseron.

(154)

To a wise man with a kyng is spedeful,   1072   If a wise man
    If his kinge do meche derogacion   sees a King
                                                 do wrong,
To hym self, his Roialme or folk vnrightful,
    To showe to hym demonstracion   he must
                                            show him, by
    Of Stories exemplificacion   1076   stories, what
                                               harm 'll come
      Playnly, that he may vnderstand the blame,   of it.
      To eschewe of mysgouernance the name.   1078

Bonos honora, ex hoc enim populi optinebis amorem ;
hec Aristotiles.

(155)

Put you in peine & deuoire euermore   1079   Honour good
    The goode men to honnour & reuerence ;   men, and
                                                  your folk 'll
And that shal encrece goodenesse more & more,   love you.

So ye shal gete louely beneuolence,

And stande in grete loue bi this wise prudence, 1083

Causyng many oon to be vertuous,

Eschewing many a werke vicious.   1085

Bone discrecionis est, & fortis animi & laudabi[li]s fidei, qui tolleret aduersitates cum venerint ; quia qualis sit homo in prosperitatibus, non probatur ; Confortare igitur ex eo quod frater est tibi, et eo quod dominus te absoluit a pestibus, et que tibi contulit non abneges dona ; hec Aristotiles.

(156)

A strong-
sould man
can suffer
adversity.

It is of goode and noble discrecioñ,   1086

And of right stronge soule & laudable,

And right of a goode feithful entencioñ,

That can suffer aduer[si]tise greueable.

Men can't be
tested in
prosperity.

That a man is, he is not prouable   1090

In prosperite, ne in felicite.

So goddes yefte forsaken wol not be.   1092

Liberalitas est concedere indigenti & merenti iuxta possibilitatem donantis ; quia qui vltra possibilitatem concedit, liberalis non est, sed vere vastator ; et qui non indigenti concedit, non est acceptus, sed est velud qui aquam spergit in mari ; hec Aristoteles.

(157)

Liberality is,
to give what
you can to
the needy.

Liberalite is a graunt to nedi   1093

And to al maner people deseruyng,

After his power there to be redy.

To graunt ouer his power is wastyng.

Giving to the
unneedy is
waste.

And who that to [un]nedy wolbe graunting,   1097

Is not accepted as for man witty,

As wastyng water in the see, gilty.   1099

Bonitatum Inicia Insipida sunt. Fine tenus vero sunt Dulcia. & prauitatum principia du[l]cia ; fine tenus vero sunt amara ; hec Plato.

(158)

Goodness is,
first, bitter ;
then sweet.

Two thinges haueth alway in mynde,   1100

The begynnyng of goodenesse is bittyr,

The ende is right swete, of natural kynde.

The begynnyng of shreudnesse[1] is swetter,

But the ende is of bitternesse the gretter. 1104

  So of goode begynnyng is goode endyng,

  And of shreudenesse comethe Il concludyng. 1106

Evil is, first, sweet; then bitter.

Ex consuetudinib*us*, vnamqua*m*q*ue* rem quidam malam reputant, quidam bonam, p*r*eter fidelitatem qua*m*
reputant omnes bonam ; h*ec* Plato.

(159)

Sum men reputen of consuetude 1107

  Euery thinge goode, & sum Il, by nature.

But euery man trouthe for goode wol conclude,

  And lengest wol laste & eke best indure,

  And to euery man metest & moost sure ; 1111

    Therfore kepith euer fidelite,

    In eschewyng sclaunderous enormyte. 1113

Some think all things good; others, all ill.

But Truth is best.

Bonor*um* bonitatem inuicem bonos cogit diligere ;
malor*um* tu*m* malicia in alios inuicem cogit odire. Nam
videre potes q*uo*d ueridicus veridicum diligit, et fidelis
fidelem. Mendax vero abhominat*ur* mendacem, et
latro latron*em* capit nullam cu*m* eo, cupiens p*ropter*
iniq*u*itatem societatem h*abe*re ; hec Plato.

(160)

The goodnesse of people[2] compellith 1114

  Goode folkes to be [to]gider lovely ;

The malice of evil men Rebelliħ,

  And makithe theime to lyve odiously.

Trewe men and feithful loue their lyk sadly ; 1118

  Lyers and theves haten iche other,

  And the toon wolde fayne vndoe the tother. 1120

Goodness brings love;

malice brings hate.

Sis legalis co*m*mittenti se tibi, & fidelis ei qui tui
gerit fiduciam, et eris securus vitandi malu*m* finem ; &
p*ropte*r veritatem et legalitatem, honorabunt te tui
amici ; et p*ropter* omittend*um* q*uo*d n*on* profuit, com-
plebit*ur* tua bonitas ; hec Socrates.

(161)

Be lauful to eu*er*yche man co*m*mitting 1121

  Hym self to you bi any submissioñ,

Keep faith with those who trust you.

---

[1] wickedness   [2] MS. pleople

And be feithful to iche man you trustyng,
 And ye shul please god in yo*ur* direccioñ,
 And be suer of billed[1] conclusion.   1125

For your truth, your friends 'll honour you.

 A[nd] for trouthe a noble legalite,
 Of yo*ur* free[n]des ye shul worshipd be. 1127

Non potes reuocare quod dixisti nec q*uo*d fecisti;
ergo prouideas ante tibi; h*e*c Socrates.

(162)

You can't recall your words or deeds.

Suche a man may nat reuoke his saying, 1128
 Ner that he hath doon w*ith* his honeste;
He hathe grete cause to make pr*o*uidyng
 Before, while he is at his liberte.
For thing doon or saide a-yenst equite, 1132
 Purchaseth vilany & dishonoure,
 Makyng many a man therfore to loure. 1134

3 pitiful things :
(1)
(2)
(3)

De tribus quib*usda*m esse pietas; quor*um* vnus est
bonus, qui est in Regimine mali et iste est[2] dolorosus
semp*er* super eo q*uo*d videt et audit; et alter est sensatus gubernatus p*er* prauu*m*, qui semp*er* est in labore
et tristicia. Tertius est liberalis, que*m* oportet petere[3]
ab auaro, q*uia* e*st* in magna angustia; h*e*c Socrates.

(163)

1. A good man to be under a bad one's rule.
2. A wise man to be under a shrew.
3. A liberal man to ask money of a miser.

Ther bene thre thinges right meche piteus : 1135
 A goode man to be longe in Regiment
Of an Il man, whiche is right dolorous;
 A wytty man to be in gouernement
 Of a shrewe,[4] disposed to il entente; 1139
 A liberal mañ, of the couetous
 To aske often meche money plentuos. 1141

3 evil things :
(1)
(2)
(3)

Incedunt male negocia hominu*m*, cu*m* bo*n*um con-
siliu*m* fue*r*it in eo qui non auditur; & Arma in eo qui
non utitur; & Diuicie in eo qui non expendit; hec
Socrates.

(164)

1. Good advice in one who isn't heard.

Thre thinges be in a right simpul knot; 1142
 First, goode counseil in hym that is not herde;

---

[1] registered [2] MS. ist. [3] MS. peterere.
[4] A wicked man, not fem. as in the next century.

And armour in hym that vsith it not;

    And Richesse in hym that kepith it herde :

Of thes thre thinges ye may be a-ferde,   1146

    But ye bestowe theim aftur their nature,

    Wisely, manly, and godly in mesure.   1148

> 2. Armour on him who doesn't use it.
> 3. Riches in one who hoards it.

Sequaris bona opera, & disce Sapienciam a melioribus qui fuerint tuo tempore, vitans laqueum quem mulieres parant viris, qui est impeditor & disturbator sapiencie, et facit assequi malum statum ; hec Socrates.

> 3 things to be observd: (1) (2) (3)

(165)

Also I wolde thre thinges ye shul kepe :   1149

    Folowe goode werkes, lerne wisdam of the best,

In love of women wade nat over depe ;

    Thus ye shul kepe you pesebly in rest,

    In goode werkes, wisdom, & lif honest,   1153

        And come to grete glory and noble fame

        Thurgh your goode liffe & vnblemyshed name.

> 1. Do good works.
> 2. Learn wisdom.
> 3. Don't be too fond of Women.

Non ponatis dona vestra nisi in locis propriis, quia plures simplices exhibent non indigentibus, sicut exhibere deberent indigentibus ; hec Socrates.

(166)

Yeve your yeiftes conueniently   1156

    To men nedy & truly deseruyng,

Not scatering your goode rechelesly,

    But after merites, withoute wastyng,

    Tendryng your folkes in your rewardyng ;   1160

        Wherof people wol haue Joy & comfort,

        And of youre high estate make goode report. 1162

> Give only to poor deserving men.

Melior est cognicio quam Ignora[n]cia / quia per cognicionem vitat quis cadere in ignem ; et per ignoranciam facit mergere in profundum ; hec Omerus.

(167)

Better is goode knowlege than Ignorance.   1163

    By knowlege, men eschewe in fire to falle ;

By ignorance, men have no wise substance,

    From depnes of drownyng helpe to calle.

    So goode & wise knowledge[1] is best of al,   1167

> Knowledge is better than Ignorance.

[1] MS. knowlelge.

Who that nougħt knowithe, litle can prouide,
Ner helpe sike when necessite betide.   1169

Iste mundus domus est m*er*cacionis ; & est infortuna-
tus ille[1] qui recedit ab eo cum p*er*dicione ; hec Omerus.

(168)

This world
is a house of
merchandise.

This world is but an house of merchandise.   1170
He is unfortunat, that vnwisely
Dep*ar*tith with losse in vntrifty wise,

Win the
best of it,
Heaven.

Sithe he may wynne heuen aduisely,
Whiche is the most best m*er*chandise iustly.   1174
Al the merchandise in this world is nough[t],
But at last to heuen he be brought.   1176

Mansuetudo eloquii aufert tedium ; hec Omerus.

(169)

A fair speaker

A feire speker with swete mansuetude   1177
Refreynethe grete noyes & displeasance,
Where rigorous Speche, vengeable & rude,
Subvertithe al polletique ordenance.
Therfore he that spekith wele in vsance,   1181

comforts
many, and
pleases Jesus.

Bothe in hym selfe & many other easithe,
And Almyghty Jesu hertly pleasith.   1183

Non extollat[ur] quis nobilitate h*a*bita diuiciis aut
dom*i*nio et voluntas dicta et op*er*a equentur ; & sic asse-
curabit de*us* eum & procedentes ab eo Successores suos ;
hec hermes.   (170)

Him who is
not puft up
by wealth or
position,

Who that wol not exalte hym for Richesse,   1184
Or for grete honno*ur* or dominacioñ,
And kepe wille, speche & werke in evenesse,

God shall
exalt.

God wol bring hym to exaltacioñ,
And his Successo*ur*s by nom*i*nacion,   1188
And theim assure in grete nobilite,
For their goode gouernance & equite.   1190

Error sapientis est sicut fraccio nauis, q*uod cum* sub-
merg*itur* ipsa, facit submergi multos ; hec hermes.

[1] MS. illi.

(171)

Therror of a wise man is in lykenesse 1191 *A wise man's mistake*
 As brekynge of a Shippe in his drownyng,
Brynging many a man to bitternesse.
 So dothe a wise man grete troble bringing *brings many folk into*
 When he is in errour, for men wenyng 1195 *trouble.*
 That a wise man guydeth, & nought eschape,
 And al is holden wisdam & no Iape. 1197

Prout decet Regiam dignitatem popu*l*um sibi commissum e*sse* obedientem ei, sic decet vt sit Rex studiosus
circa statu*m* eoru*m* prius qua*m* circa statu*m* suu*m*, q*u*ia
sic est ip*s*e penes eos, sicut a*n*i*m*a penes corp*us*, hec
Hermes.

(172)

As it semeth the kinges dignite 1198 *As people obey the*
 To haue of his people obedience, *King,*
Right so is accordynge of equite
 That the kinge do daily trewe diligence *he should seek their*
 To tendre thair astate w*it*h his prudence, 1202 *good before his own.*
 Rather than his owne; & euen for why
 They bene hym so nygh as sowle & body. 1204

Qui incedit cu*m* mu*n*do se*cundu*m sui disposi*c*ionem
no*n* est requirendus ad danda consilia, q*u*ia non dabit
nisi arbitrio voluntatis, p*ro* eo q*uo*d illius qui non mutatur mu[n]dum est amor intellectualis, et mutantis eum
est Amor voluntarius; hec Socrates.

(173)

A worldly man in dispo*s*icioñ, 1205 *A worldly self-seeking*
 Folowyng the worlde daily in his mynde, *man can't be trusted to*
May not be of feithful entencioñ *give good counsel.*
 To yeve trewe & iust counseil in his kynde.
 For aftur his wille he wol hym selfe finde, 1209
 And eu*er*y thinge determen wilfully,
 Aye[n]ste Reason, & eke vnskilfully. 1211

Si volueris q*uo*d non erret tuus filius vel seruus, Id
queras quod est ex*tra* naturam; hec Pitagagoras (*sic*).

(174)

Don't expect
that your son
or servant 'll
never go
wrong.

Yef ye haue in your hert a volunte   1212

   To[1] your sonne or servaunt er not foly, .

Ye must be in that liberalite

   To seke a thing a-ye[n]st nature truly ;

   For no man can be so perfite Iustly,   1216

     But he is at somme tyme fallible,

     And at summe tyme right goode & credible. 1218

Securior est homo ex silencio quam ex multi-loquio, quia per l[o]cuciones potest incedi in errores. hoc non contingit scienti quid loquitur, sed ignorans errat qui loqui vult profilue aut diminute. Et commodum tacendi est magis commodo loquendi. Et dampnum loquendi magis est dampno tacendi. Et sensatus cognoscitur ex multa taciturnitate, & ignorans ex multa loquacitate. Et qui per se non tacet, cogetur tacere per alium, & minus appreciabitur. Et qui tacet donec ad loquendum inducatur, est melior eo qui loquitur, donec tacere mandetur, loqucio est in posse hominis donec donec (*sic*) loquitur, & deinde euadit a posse Ipsius. Et si homo loquitur, cognoscitur si est perfectus aut diminutus ; et si tacet, dubitatur qualis sit. Et qui vult loqui, prius consideret aspiciat suum verbum ; quia melius est quod ipse suspiciat quam alter. Et eloquium tuum audietur, ergo nitaris recte pronunciare, aut taceas. Et qui tacet, scrutatur eloquia aliorum. Et qui dolet, ex eloquio assecuratur, quod sit percussus ; hec Socrates.

(175)

Silence is
better than
speech.

To profit, to be stille is more profit   1219

   Thanne to speke ; & harme to speke more damage

Thanne te be stille, & grettir discomfit.

A wise man
speaks little.

To speke litil, is knowen a man sage ;

   To speke meche, is knowen a man in Rage.   1223

     Whan a mañ spekith, his wit is knoweñ,

     To be stille, doubte is how it[2] shal be blowen.

Utere bonis moribus & diligeris, et licet sis turpis, pulcritudo morum superabit sanctificacione[3] figurarum. Hec Socrates.

  [1] ? That   [2] MS. is it..   [3] MS. sanctificacionem.

(176)

Man vsing goode maners, shal be Loued 1226 — A man of good manners is lov'd.
 Amonges goode men & honourable ;
And thaugh he be foule and diffugured (*sic*), — Even if he is ugly, his fine manners shall win him praise.
 The beaute of his maners commendable
Shal ouercome al other Reproueable. 1230
 And his figure in Recommendacioñ
Shal be had, and in Laudacioñ. 1232

Qui amore mundi suam a*n*i*m*am replet, tribus replet ea*m*, *scilicet*, paupe*r*tate qua*m* nunqu*am* vitabit, vt di-uicias contingat; & fiducia, que numq*uam* peruenit ad fine*m* ; et impedimento[1] sine expedicione. Hec Socrates.

(177)

Who that wolbe worldly, & it louynge, 1233 — The worldly man shall reap poverty,
 Thre defaultes he shal haue eue*r*more :
In grete pouerte, for Riches sekynge ;
 In truste, whiche shal neu*er* come to end therf[or]e ; — disappointment, and hindrance.
 And in gre[t] impediment more & more, 1237
  Whiche shal neuer haue expedicion.
 This is sothe, w*ith*-oute any question. 1239

Non e*st* paciens q*ui* ta*m* gravatus est qua*m* tollerare potuit, & sustinuit illud, sed ille qui grauatus est ultra possibilitate*m* sue nature, et sustinuit illud ; hec Pitagoras.

(178)

Thus ye shul knowe a man in pacience, 1240 — The patient man suffers hardship patiently.
 þat is greued ayenst possibilite
Of nature, and it sufferith w*ith* prudence.
 But he that is greued in adue*r*site,
 And may wele bere it in his freilte, 1244
  In no wise may be clept pacient
 By this descripcioñ or Iugement. 1246

Non quiescatis ve*st*ris ope*r*ibus in optinendis magnis delectacionibus, q*ui*a sustinere no*n* poteris adue*r*sitates cum venerint ; hec Pitagoras.

[1] MS. impedimentu*m*.

O 2

(179)

Don't live
luxuriously,

Kepe neuer yo*ur* body delectably,   1247
     Not in softe lyinge, ne delicacye,

or you'll
not be able
to bear
adversity.

For ye may nat suffre reasonably
     Aduersite, ne it fortifie,
       Ner in no man*er* wise it iustifie.   1251
       Therfore be nat meche ouer curious
       In delicacie, ne delicious.   1253

Adquesce tuis aurib*us*, nam *pro*pter ea, Habuisti duas aures, & os vnu*m*, vt plus audias qu*am* loqu*ar*is; hec Diogenes.

(180)

You have 2
ears and
1 mouth, that
you may
listen, and
not talk too
much.

Euery man hathe oon Mouthe & two eres,   1254
     To thentente that he sholde here more[1] thanne speke.
To speke meche, many people-is deres;
     To here many thinges, & to be meke,
       Right meche wisdam & w*er*tue it dothe seke.   1258
       So, in litil speche & right meche heryng,
       Many grete v*er*tues is conquering.   1260

Non confidas in mu*n*do, q*ui*a numquam soluit quod promissit *pre*decessorib*us*; & idem faciet tibi.   Hec Socrates.

(181)

Trust not in
the World,
for it does
not fulfil its
promise.

Lete never[2] man putte in ful confdence   1261
     In the world, for he maketh no p[ay]ment
Of his *pro*misse, but so in negligence

[*MS. imperfect.*]

---

[1] MS. more more.   [2] MS. nerv*er*.

LIST OF WORDS

(By F. J. FURNIVALL).

a, *a.* 21/258, one
abydy, *v.i.* 17/145, abide
Active Policy of a Prince, p. 12—41
advisinesse, 17/137, 31/577, due consideration
alther, our, 8/229, 16/119, of us all
and, *conj.* 54/268, if
antiquaile, *n.* 75/724, oldness, age
appliable, *a.* 24/367, 28/474, 87/984, attentive, submissive
arect, *v.t.* 11/329, assign, impute
areryng, *n.* 76/740, rising
Ashby, George, put into the Fleet Prison, 1/8; plunderd, 1/20-1; his name, 2/29; at Henry VI's court, 3/58; Writer to the Signet, 3/64; his 'Reflections' written in prison, A.D. 1463, 11/337-8; prays God for help, his English is so bad, p. 14
ass-head, *n.* 30/564, stupid
associe, *v.t.* 72/645, associate
assurance, *n.* 44/40, 48/130, security
awaken, *p.pl.* 20/234, kept alive?
awakyn, *v.i.* 1/19, pounce

bad, *a.* 3/77, destitute, poor
be *for* but, *conj.* 38/590
bear the bell, 33/645
benevolence, *n.* 36/738, good will
bill of complaint, 31/577
billed, *a.* 94/1129, registered
blabber, *n.* 77/772, teller of secrets
blabbynge, *n.* 32/624
blessedly, *adv.* 79/795
blondryng, *pl.* 14/26, blundering
blustering, *pl.* 1/3
blyyn, *v.i.* 8/235, cease
bringing-up, *n.* 2/22, 79/809, nurture
butts for archery, every town to have, 31/572
buxom, *a.* 41/899, obedient

castigation, *n.* 12/347
cast me, *vb.* 4/96, design
censualyte, 6/171, sensuality
change of high estates, 18/169
chargeable, *a.* 27/455, responsible
Chaucer, 13/1
childred = children, 71/631
clarified (metal), *p.pl.* 5/142; '(from sin), 8/234
cloth-making needs revival, 29/527
coarted, *p.pl.* 64/482, forst
commonalty not to be trusted, 40/870
complacence, *n.* 27/453, gratification
conable, *a.* 82/881, fit, proper
conceite, *n.* 36/737, favour
confidende *for* confidence, *n.* 68/582
coniectour, *n.* 34/673, contriver
constance, *n.* 34/676, constancy
consuetude, *n.* 52/207, temper
consyderall, *n.* 4/102, consideration
coraging, *p.pl.* 45/69, encouraging
coronation, *n.* 26/419, right to the Crown
costlowe, *a.* 91/1066, costly
couetise, *n.* 19/198, covetousness
crakyng, *n.* 79/803, crying out, distress
cronicle, *v.t.* and *n.* 18/151, 155, 25/392, 26/437
crook, *n.* 26/407, trick

delate, 14/54, dilate, spin out
demert, demeryt, *n.* 5/121, 136, demerit
departith, *v.t.* 29/514, separates
dependour, *n.* 78/791, dependence, want
dere, *n.* 14/49, injury
deres, *v.i.* 100/1256, injures
derogacion, *n.* 91/1073

desert, *n.* 5/123, deserving
despeccion, 78/782, contempt
devoid, *v.t.* 19/191, shunt, dismiss
deynous, *a.* 39/843, disdainful
Dicta Philosophorum, p. 42—100
dilapidation, *n.* 23/316
disclaundre, *n.* 27/438, disrepute
discuss, *v.t.* 2/28, beat out, search out
disguised, *a.* 39/843, hypocritical
displeasance, *n.* 49/135
disseure, *v.t.* 53/244, dissever, separate
dissever, *v.t.* 22/292, separate
dissimile, *v.i.* 51/183, dissemble
doer, good, 48/128, benefactor
doon-to, *p.pl.* 48/131, treated
draught, *n.* 2/22, 28/471, education
dronkelowe, *a.* 72/646, drunken
dronkship, *n.* 59/373, drunkenness
dud, *v.aux.* 18/157, dudde, *pl.* 19/210, did
due, *a.* 25/393, rightful
dysease, *n.* 2/34, 6/149, mishap, ill fate
dyseasyd, *p.t.* 3/81, troubled, injured

Edward IV, 16/92
egression, *n.* 13/16, exit, death
elevate, *a.* 18/164, exalted
enchaunced, *p.pl.* 40/891, 55/284, 58/339, exalted
english, *n.* 13/3, 5, E. language
———, *v.t.* 13/21, 14/37, translate into E.
entremete, *v.i.* 16/107, intermeddle
equivolent, *a.* 33/657, of equal force
erudicion, *n.* 48/129, doctrine
exaltatat, *v.t.* 32/614, exalt, glorify
executor, *n.* 22/303, performer, carrier out
exemplification, *n.* 91/1076
exorn, *v.t.* 86/953, adorn

fair wife, a, 6/167
falseness, *n.* 19/200
felle, *n.* 64/487, cruelty
fere, *v.t.* 49/140, frighten
feruein, *a.* 66/529, fervent, burning
fitting, *a.* 59/361, suitable
Fleet Prison, 1/8
foolship, *n.* 49/149, 52/225, folly
formacion, 13/5, making, writing
formal, *a.* 29/521, due
fresh, *a.* 39/843, frank

frivolly, *adv.* 31/581, frivolously

geasen, *n.* 85/943, scarcity
Gloucester, Humfrey, Duke of, 3/61
go where he go, 19/201
God's law and will, 20/239, 240
Gower, 13/1
grauntyng, *n.* 35/724, giving, bestowing
gre, *n.* 9/252, 10/279, ease, pleasure
greable, *adj.* 4/104, agreeable, pleasing
greueable, *a.* 92/1089, grievous, painful
grogyng, *a.* 6/154, grudging
guiding, *n.* 37/775, 39/330, 51/177, 71/644

handlyng, *n.* 2/25, hands
Henry VI and his Queen, 3/60, 16/94-5
hynde, *v.t.* 57/329, hinder

ie, *n.* 39/857, eye
ill-disposed, *n.* 73/671
ill nature, of, 72/646
imprisonment, *n.* 2/46
incorrigible, *a.* 52/214, extravagant
indifferent, *a.* 33/656, impartial
indisposed, *a.* 17/135, not inclined; ill-disposed, 57/327
inicion, *n.* 38/819, start, beginning
insenced, *p.pl.* 38/827, disposed ?, informd ?
inspection, *n.* 22/287, 25/377, 27/467, 37/775, 44/31
instance, *n.* 73/676, urgency
intellection, *n.* 25/391, 35/720, understanding, information
intential, *a.* 14/39, of the author's meaning
inventive, *a.* 13/12
ireful, *a.* 54/269, angry
-is, *gen.* with -s: sowles is helthe, 27/464; roialmes is destruccion, 68/574
-is, *pl.* people -is, folk, 100/1256

jape, *n.* 26/414, joke, jest
Job, 9/246
John the Baptist, 8/241
——— Evangelist, 8/239
justify, *v.t.* 20/220, do justice ?

knet, *p.pl.* 38/816, combined, joind ?

knot, *n.* 94/1142
kynde, *n.* 48/122, nature, birth

laborous, *a.* 69/591, 87/990, 89/1033, industrious
Labourers, Statute of, 30/539
lance, 30/541
largeness, *n.* 84/908, liberality
lastingly, *adv.* 40/892
laudacion, *n.* 99/1232, praising
law of Nature, 34/696
led, *n.* 5/121, the metal lead
lesion, *n.* 72/659, injury
lesure, *n.* 13/21, injury?
lesyng, *ppl.* 6/175, losing
lesyngmonger, 72/652, liar
letter, *n.* 64/474, stopper, preventer
lettred, *p.pl.* 33/648, 651, educated
levelode, livelode, *n.* 59/374, 377, livelihood
liberality, *n.* 98/1214
licencing, *a.* 76/739, giving leave
ligeance, *n.* 26/425, allegiance
lineally, *adv.* 15/86
lite, *n.* 38/813, little
lord, folks' wish to be one, 27/450
lure, *n.* 9/269, trap, snare
Lydgate, 13/1
lyme, *v.t.* 87/983, limit?

maker, *n.* 32/613, poet
makyng, *n.* 12/341, 13/14, composition, poem
makyng, 35/731, benefit, advancement
malices, *n.pl.* 7/201
mandement, *n.* 33/654, 52/204, giving orders
mansuetude, *n.* 40/880, 52/205, gentleness
Margaret of Anjou, Queen of Henry VI, 3/60, 16/95
Mary, the Queen of Heaven, 8/232
meane, *a.* 38/809, middle-class
medle, *vb.* 33/655, mix
me thynketh, 4/92, 97, it seems to me
merytory, *a.* 7/210, 10/301, meritorious
minishing, *n.* 14/32, lessening, omission
mischance, *n.* 44/47
mischeue, *v.i.* 36/753, do mischief
misericorde, *n.* 35/700, 37/784, mercy

misgovernance, 37/797
misgoverned, *a.* 62/438
misguiding, *n.* 26/431, 64/494
misrule, *n.* 26/430 ; *v.t.* 43/19
misruled, *n.* 19/213
miswent, *p.pl.* 63/469, gone wrong
most clennyst, *a.* 8/233
mule, *n.* 30/564
Myghelmas, 1/6, Michaelmas

nedeful, *a.* 6/156
noblay, *n.* 64/477, noble state
nomination, *n.* 21/257, 45/54, 52/213, 96/1188, reputation?
noy, *n.* 4/95, annoyance
noyant, *a.* 74/699, injurious
nycyte, *n.* 53/243, folly
nygonship, *n.* 67/548, niggardliness

obeiceantly, *adv.* 33/652, obediently
oblivion, *n.* 33/637
observant, *a.* 30/560
odiously, *adv.* 93/1117
of, *prep.* 10/300, by means of, through ; 12/349, from
old : After the old dog, the young whelp barks, 32/615
omnipotency, *n.* 20/218
opportune, *a.* 24/357, gracious
opteyne, *v.t.* 8/238, obtain
ostend, *v.t.* 15/56, show
other-whyle, *adv.* 4/107, 111, sometimes
overgoon, *p.pl.* 28/498, past over
over-ride, *v.t.* 58/341

pacificie, *v.t.* 81/841, appease
patientness, *n.* 23/326
pay, *n.* 35/705, pleasure, satisfaction
payment, *n.* 100/1262, fulfilment
pen and ink, 3/68
perisshed, *p.pl.* 36/736, distrest
perpetuity, *n.* 66/540, everlastingness
pleies, *n.pl.* 31/571, games
plentuously, *adv.* 33/646
plucker-at, *n.* 7/193, envier, one who tries to pull down another
politic, *a.* 19/210, 50/168, 88/1004, 96/1180, prudent
polleci, *n.* 33/643, policy
positive law, 34/695
pourely, *adv.* 70/612, miserably, in poverty
poverty parts fellowship, 29/514

spoylyng, *n.* 2/23, plundering, robbery

spring, *v.t.* 36/747, spread, diffuse

spyrytualyte, *n.* 7/182, religion, clerical office

Statute of Labourers, 37 Edw. III, c. 8-14, 30/540; of Weapons, 2 Edw. III, c. 3, 30/526

sterve, *v.i.* 19/192, perish

straitly, *adv.* 50/163, strictly

streit, *a.* 21/253, strict

strumpery, *n.* 29/533, strumpetry

subversion, *n.* 37/793

suppressing, *n.* 26/417

supprise, *v.t.* 60/396, suppress, put down

surance, *n.* 25/357, 30/549, safety

surmonte, *v.i.* 60/397, rise up

takyng, *n.* 36/734, accepting, possessing

temporalyte, *n.* 7/181, worldly business

temps, *n.* 25/375, time

tendryng, *ppl.* 95/1160, favouring

tene, *n.* 4/87, 8/236, grief

terrestrial, *a.* 31/592, dwelling on earth

thank, *v.t.* 84/925, say thanks for

that, ? *v. aux.* 74/703, does

thee, *v.i.* 21/255, thrive

then, *conj.* 5/147, than

thoutfull, *a.* 6/170, anxious

threted, *p.pl.* 56/308, threatened

tiranship, *n.* 23/332, tyranny

to, with *vb.* tespie, 40/860 ; toptaine, 40/869; tobaie, 80/830, &c.

tongue breaks bones, 64/489

transitory, *a.* 8/220

translation, *n.* 18/156, transference, ill change

treuleche, 32/621, truly

trice, *n.* 69/598, station in hunting

triumphal, *a.* 7/209

trowbelous, *a.* 9/250, troubled, afflicted

tuicion, *n.* 33/666, guardianship

unadvised, *a.* 59/385

unblemisht, *a.* 64/479, 95/1155

under, *adv.* 10/292, as an underling

uncunning, *n.* 82/864, ignorance

unfitting, *a.* 3/74, 58/359, rude, coarse, unsuitable

unfriend, *n.* 83/885

union, *n.* 74/703, unity

universal, *a.* 37/772

universally, *adv.* 37/788

unkunnyng, *n.* 66/534, 73/670, ignorant folk

unpayable, *a.* 2/44

unportable, *a.* 18/172, unbearable

unrest, *n.* 59/371

unrightful, 91/1074

unsemyng, *a.* 86/967, unfitting

unskilfully, *adv.* 97/1211, unreasonably

unthe, *v.i.* 23/330, 78/784, not thrive, come to grief

unthrift, *n.* 63/469, unthriftiness

unthriftiness, *n.* 48/116

unthrifty, *a.* 34/681, mean

unwise, *a.* 25/404

upbrought, *p.pl.* 28/473, brought up, nurtured

upon, *prep.* 33/668, over: reign upon us

utterance, *n.* 49/154, speaking

utterest, *a.* 24/371 ; to the ut., 50/162

vailable, *a.* 28/475, suitable

vale, *n.* 65/501 (L. *parvi*), downflow, runlet ?

verrey, *a.* 53/245, true

vertuest, *a.* 28/480, most virtuous

vesture, *n.* 29/535, clothing, dress

vilipend, *v.t.* 16/105

volunte, *n.* 7/202, 12/350, 98/1212, will

wade, *v.i.* 14/46

wakyng, *a.* 75/715, watching

wasting, *a.* 92/1096

web, *n.* 25/379, foundation, ground

well-aged, 38/815

well-disposed, *a.* 22/307, 67/567

well in goodes, 3/78, well off

well-manered, *a.* 48/113

well-ruled, *n.* 19/214

well-willed, *a.* 63/450

well-willer, *n.* 26/422

whirlyng, *ppl.* 54/259

wiles croke, 26/407, trick of deceit

wo worthe ! 34/688-94, woe be to !

wrongfully, *adv.* 2/52

wyte, *v.t.* 5/125, impute, blame

wytti, *v.t.* 36/741, skilful ; 73/666, wise